DO YOUR OWN THING WITH MACRAMÉ

DO YOUR OWN THING WITH MACRAMÉ

by Lura LaBarge

WATSON-GUPTILL, NEW YORK

PITMAN PUBLISHING, LONDON

First published 1973 in the United States and Canada by Watson-Guptill Publications,
a division of Billboard Publications, Inc.,
1515 Broadway, New York, N.Y. 10036

Published simultaneously in Great Britain by Sir Isaac Pitman & Sons Ltd.,
39 Parker Street, Kingsway, London WC2B 5PB
ISBN 0-273-00258-9

Library of Congress Cataloging in Publication Data
LaBarge, Lura.
    Do Your Own Thing With Macrame.
    Bibliography: p.
    1. Macrame.   I. Title.
TT840.L3   1973   746.44   73-644
ISBN 0-8230-1354-5

Manufactured in Japan

First Printing, 1973
Second Printing, 1974
Third Printing, 1976
Fourth Printing, 1977

To Leo M. and Leo R.

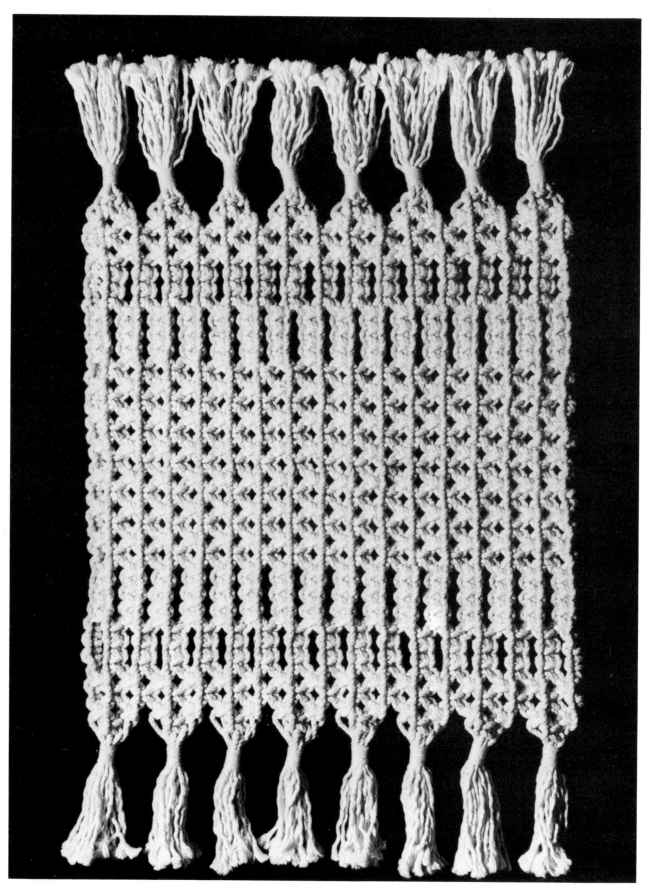

The ribbed effect in this seat mat was produced by reversing the direction of the square knotting in each alternating row. Worked by the author for *Lady's Circle Magazine*.

Acknowledgments

I would like to thank George Pfiffner, who encouraged me to go ahead with the book in the first place, and Anthony E. Kropilak, who provided both his technical expertise and many of the designs seen throughout the book. I also want to thank Lawrence L. Schroth, Jr. and Geoffrey Clements, who took all the color photographs; my students and friends, who offered their macramé for photographing; and finally, Jennifer Place, my editor.

An imaginative hanging combining twisted sennits and handmade pottery pieces. The hanging was designed and worked by Anthony E. Kropilak.

Contents

Introduction

In writing this book I've assumed the reader wishes to learn enough about macramé to design his own original projects. There are macramé books that take the inspirational approach, showing pictures of what other artists have done and giving a few hints on how they did it. Then there are books that take the pattern approach, offering projects complete with step-by-step instructions that permit the reader to produce exact duplicates. I've chosen a third scheme that might be considered the logical A-B-C approach—mechanics first, then materials and esthetics. This book aims at all times to stimulate the reader's own individual design instincts, to show the way rather than to lead the march.

In working out original concepts in macramé there are few rules. You can really do your own thing: you can work freely or tightly; in gaudy, shiny colors or soft, natural tones; adhere strictly to macramé knots or introduce fancy ropework or woven parts; embellish your work with pottery, wood, metal, ceramics, plastic, or a collection of found objects; make a functional piece or a freeform, fanciful work of art.

You can approach learning the knots two ways. You can look at the photographs, note which items are suggested projects, and make one, "learning" each knot as you come to it. Or you can cut some lengths of cord and start to practice. Actually, a combination of the two is probably the most rewarding way of going at it—practice a bit, then make something useful or decorative in a cord you select for that project.

There is a lot to be said for making a learner's "quipi,"

or sampler, of your practice knots. South American Indians used a quipi as a memory aid in relaying and recording numerical information. In its simplest form the quipi consists of a main cord from which hang many dependent, knotted, colored cords, usually in groups of four. You might adapt this form for your sampler or you might decide to make up a series of sample sennits (meaningless to anyone but you, unless you label each one carefully). One way or another, the only way to learn knot tying is to tie knots.

All you'll need for making a basic sample are a ball of #36 cotton seine twine, a pair of scissors, a dozen T-pins, and a piece of Homasote about 8″ x 12″ (or a reasonable substitute) for a knotting board. You'll add to this list as you go on—probably white glue and a yarn needle, more T-pins, steel tape or a tape measure, C-clamps or a warp board for measuring cords, graph paper and pencil, scratch paper for arithmetic, and, of course, a great variety of other cords as well as embellishments such as beads to use in your macramé designs.

Macramé knots and projects can be as simple or as complicated as you want to make them, project materials can be as expensive or as inexpensive as you wish. Time is the one thing macramé does demand. It's not a quick, paint-by-numbers-and-get-done-fast pastime. But there's no sense in making a mystery out of it. Almost everyone has knotted the end of a cord and tightened it, or taken two ends of thread or cord and knotted them together without giving it a second thought. Name that the "overhand knot" and you're ready for Chapter 1!

1. Square Knots

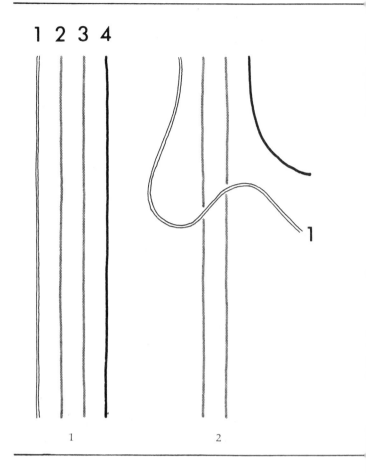

1 2 3 4

1

2

The best way to learn about macramé is to start right in. If beginning and ending your macramé project presents problems, start in the middle! That's what we intend to do here.

You'll find there are just two basic knots that you really need: *the square knot* and the *half hitch.* Variations and combinations of these two knots account for about 95% of the knotting worked in almost any collection of macramé pieces. First, let's learn to make the half knot, the first step in learning to make the square knot.

The Half Knot

The first knot to learn is the half knot. Pin four lengths of cord to your knotting surface. Numbering from left to right, #1 is the left-hand knotting cord, #2 and #3 are the core cords, and #4 is the right-hand knotting cord (1).

Half Knot to the Right. Take cord #1 and lay it across #2 and #3, leaving a loop at the left as shown (2). Then take cord #4, bring it over #1, behind #3 and #2, and through the loop, over cord #1 (3). Tighten the knot (4).

Now, do it again. The left-hand cord over, leaving the loop (5), the right-hand cord over the left, under and behind the core cords and through the loop (6). Tighten up against the first half knot (7).

If you keep this up for, say, five more knots, you'll find the sennit (a braid or chain made with a repeated pattern of knots) tends to twist, which is just great (8). That's how those involved looking spirals featured in so many macramé designs are made. Such a spiral can be seen in the stuffed hanging (9). The two core cords should be held flat and taut to prevent their twisting around each other. Turn the whole sennit (all four cords) over about every 6th or 7th knot to keep it spiraling evenly.

Half Knot to the Left. This is just the reverse: it's easy to see if the four cords are pinned in position and numbered again from left to right. This time, carry cord #4 to the left over #3 and #2, leaving a loop at the right-hand side (10). Take cord #1 over #4, behind #2 and #3, and through the loop, going over cord #4 (11). Tighten the knot and do six more. The spiral will form automatically in the opposite direction (12).

For practice, it's a good idea to knot two sennits parallel to each other, watching the work for neatness and evenness. Learn to control the tension—how tightly you tie and how evenly you push each knot up against the previous one. These are the habits that will distinguish good craftsmanship from bad.

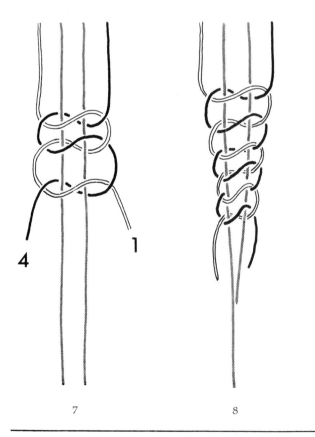

4

1

7

8

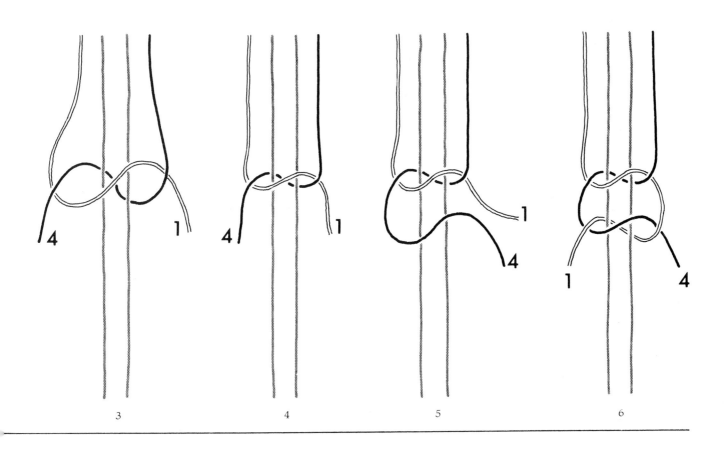

3

4

5

6

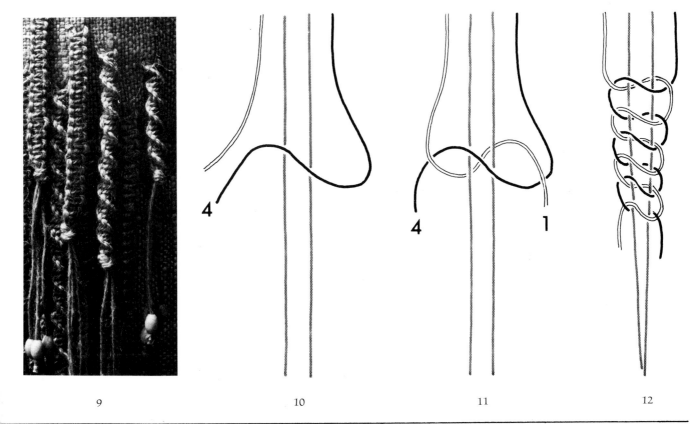

9

10

11

12

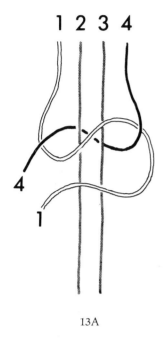

1 2 3 4

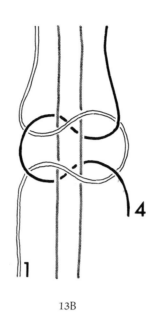

4

1

13A

4

1

13B

Nubbin

13C

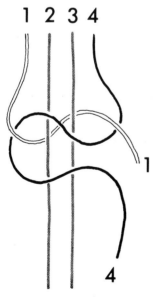

1 2 3 4

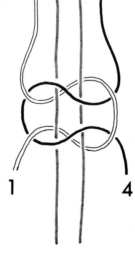

1

4

14A

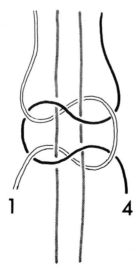

1

4

14B

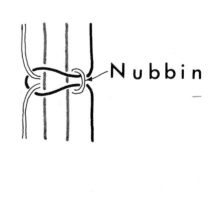

Nubbin

14C

The Square Knot

On to the square knot. You already know the two half knots, one to the right and one to the left: combining them makes a square knot (13).

Square Knot to the Right. With the four cords pinned down as before, carry cord #1 to the right, over the core cords #2 and #3, leaving a loop at the left. Take cord #4 over it, behind the core cords #3 and #2, through the loop, over #1, and down. So far, we've got a half knot to the right. Now carry cord #1 back across to the left, leaving a loop at the right and take cord #4 over #1, behind the core cords #2 and #3, and through the loop. Seem familiar? Now we've got a half knot to the left. Tighten up the knot evenly and we've made a square knot to the right.

Square Knot to the Left. Make a half knot to the left first and then a half knot to the right (14). Tighten the knot up evenly and compare with the square knot to the right. Notice the position of the nubbin (that portion of the cord seen as a loop at the side of the tightened, completed square knot) in each. Study this carefully because you'll want to remember how the difference was accomplished. When you work symmetrically, the right-hand and left-hand versions of the square knot must be remembered. In a straight square knot sennit it's impossible to tell, once you've done the whole thing, whether the middle is a right- or a left-hand knot without counting the half knots. It does show up plainly if you're using working cords of different colors, however.

Here's a hint that will help you remember which half knot to tie next if you're interrupted in your work: The strand aimed *away* from you, underneath the last completed nubbin, is the one to bring across next, leaving it looped for the other end to come through.

Sennit Variations

There are many variations in a 4-strand square knot sennit. First, you can vary the spacing. The most obvious way is to leave no space at all between knots.

Vary the Spacing. Place pins at regular intervals between the two core cords to give you a guide for spacing the knots in your sennit (15). You can tie a set number of knots tightly, then leave a set space and repeat the pattern. Or you can tie all your square knots to the right or all to the left. Or you can alternate right-hand and left-hand knots.

Another interesting thing to know about half and square knot sennits is that the knots will slide up the core cords. Try a sennit of square knots spaced 2″ apart. Make sure the two core cords are anchored well at the top, hold them taut, and slide the square knots up the core cords (16). You'll get a row of loops on both sides. Tighten each

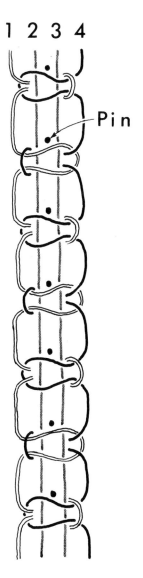

1 2 3 4

Pin

15

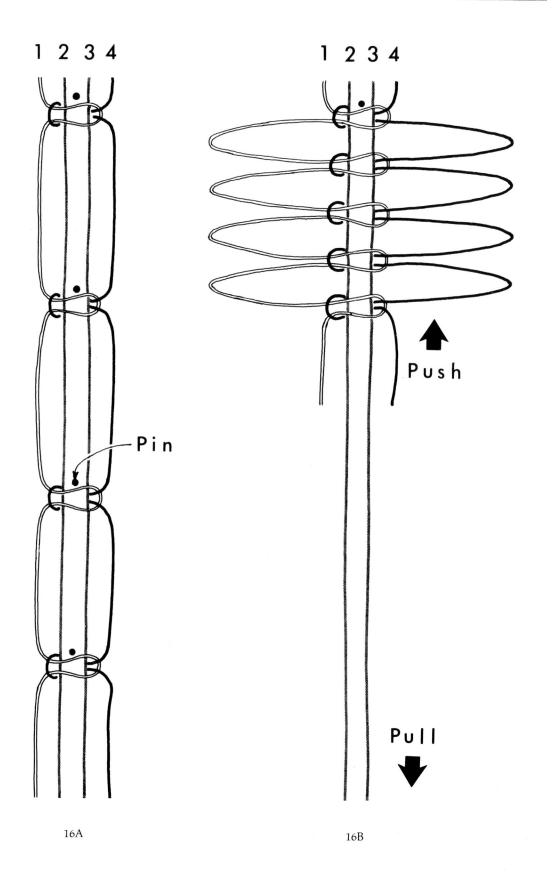

16A

16B

knot. Think about using this as a choker or fancy trim to be sewn on a sweater. Again, you can tie a sennit of square knots tightly and space out just one to slide up. This loopy knot is usually called a "butterfly" knot. It's also possible to get loops on only one side of the core, a "one-winged" butterfly (17). Let each loop go around a pin at one side of the sennit as you form the knots. You can't slide a one-winged butterfly, and it's not a very secure knot, but the idea is often useful.

Exchange Core Cords for Working Cords. Here is another variation on the square knot sennit, still using only four strands (18). Tie one square knot to the right with cords #1 and #4 over the core cords #2 and #3. Now place the #1 and #4 cords in the core position and tie another square knot with the #2 and #3 cords as the working cords over #1 and #4 as the core cords. When you place the working cords into the core position to tie the next knot, if you do it in a consistent manner—always on top or always on the bottom—you get a better looking sennit. You may want to try this in two colors of cord, the original core cords in one color, the original working cords in another. If you alternate the positioning so that the core color is always on the bottom or always on the top, you'll get a slightly different effect.

Combine Half Knots and Square Knots. Since all macramé is a combination of knots, let's see what happens when we combine a few. Try a half knot to the right with a square knot to the left (19). Try a square knot to the right with a half knot to the left. Either way, it turns out the same and it's mighty handy when working with cords that tend to slip and slide. The extra half knot often seems to give the necessary extra grip to keep the loops intact. Another variation has a more symmetrical look. Try a half knot to the right with a square knot to the right followed by a half knot to the left. Space and alternate that with a half knot to the left, with a square knot to the left followed by a half knot to the right. You might also use two half knots instead of one flanking each square knot for a more pronounced, wave-like sennit. These can also be tied tightly for still other effects.

Vary the Number of Strands. There's no rule that says you have to use four strands in a sennit, though most macramé pieces are based on four strands and multiples of four. You can tie a square knot over a single core cord within the 4-strand sennit. For a delicate sash or necklace, try tying with #1 and #3 over the core cord #2, then leave a space and tie a square knot with #2 and #4 over the core cord #3 (20). This is especially effective in heavy braided nylon, metallic cord, or anything with sufficient body to keep the arcs more or less stiff.

There's also no rule that says you have to tie knots with a single strand. You can use double or triple strands for the working cord elements or any number of strands for the core cords (21). The knots are all tied in exactly the same way.

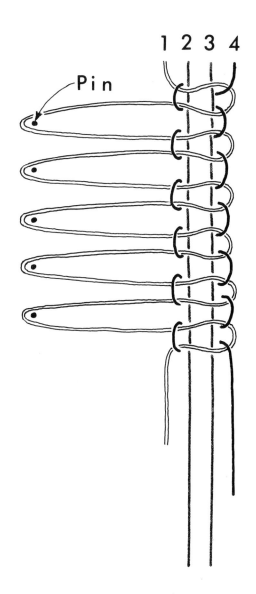

17

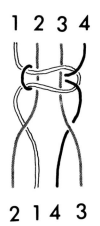

18A   18B   18C   19

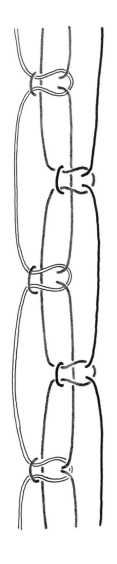

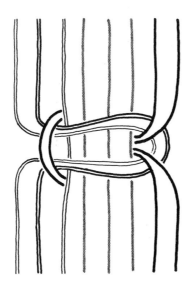

1 2 3 4 5 6 7 8

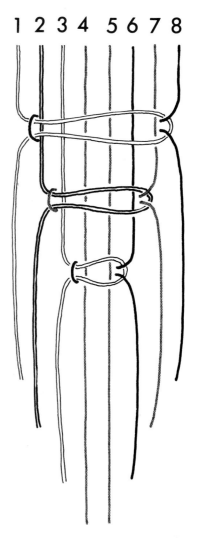

20

21

22

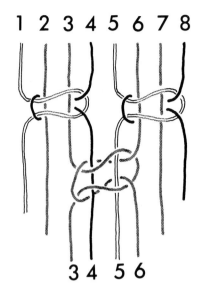

1 2 3 4 5 6 7 8

3 4 5 6

23

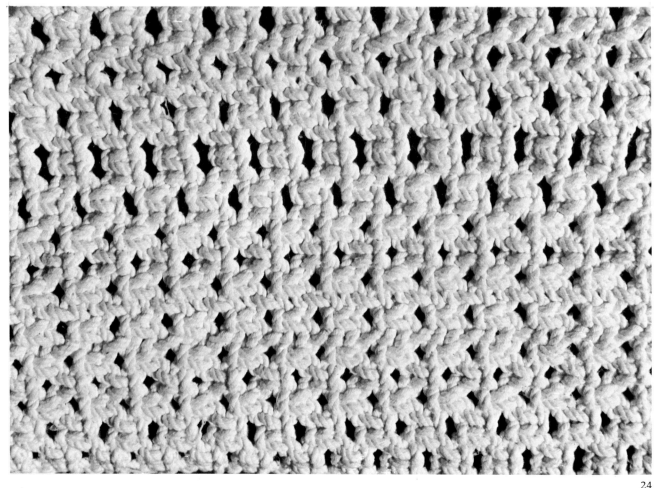

24

This kind of gathering knot can be used alone, included in a design, or as an accent; or the idea can be utilized in working out a repeat pattern. It's necessary, however, to consider your materials, because not all cords lend themselves to pairing or multiple strand use. Rug yarn can be used as a multiple core material with very satisfactory results but won't easily lay paired for the working cords. Tubular braided nylon pairs nicely and lays flat but becomes quite bulky if you use a number of strands in the core position.

The next step is to try some 8-strand variations, still using only the square knot. Tie a square knot, using #1 and #8 knotted over the core cords #2, #3, #4, #5, #6, and #7. Then tie a square knot using #2 and #7 over the core cords #3, #4, #5 and #6; then tie a square knot using #3 and #6 over the core cords #4 and #5 (22). Play around with this theme if you like, reversing the order, reversing the square knot direction, or changing the spacing.

The Alternating Square Knot

The alternating square knot forms the basis of the sailor's old square-knotting work, and understanding how it works is very important to all your future projects. Use eight strands, numbering from the left 1 through 8. With cords #1 and #4 as the working cords, tie a square knot to the right over the core cords #2 and #3. With strands #5 and #8, tie a square knot to the right over the core cords #6 and #7, placing the knots beside each other. Now, disregard cords #1 and #2 on the left and #7 and #8 on the right. Using cords #3 and #6 as the working cords, tie one square knot to the right over the core cords #4 and #5. This holds the two previous knots together (23).

Continue to alternate the two positionings within eight strands as shown and you can begin to see the endless possibilities ahead. Obviously you can use any multiple of four strands and of course you can tie more than one knot in each set of four strands.

They don't have to be square knots either. In the mat shown in the photo (24) half knots in alternating directions are connected by square knots in the 3, 4, 5, 6 cord position.

Square knot sennits of unequal lengths can be joined by a square knot in the alternating position, as well (25).

Sennit Projects

What can you do with just a sennit? You can make a sash, choker, bookmark, headband, hatband, handles for drawers, or a strong "string" for your skate key. With 8, 12, or more strands to work with and the idea of the alternating square knot, many more design possibilities appear. Utilization of what we've already covered is shown in the 12-strand square-knotted belt (26). Trios of

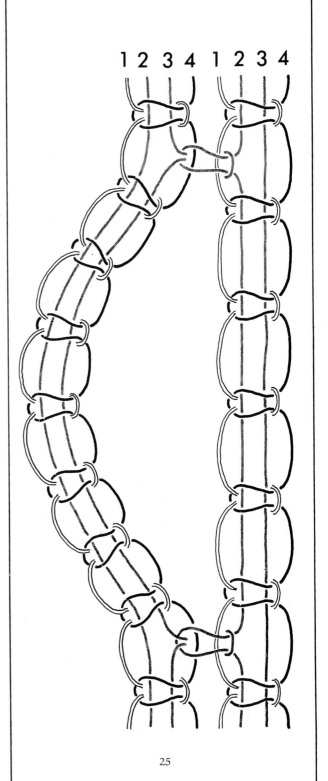

1 2 3 4 1 2 3 4

25

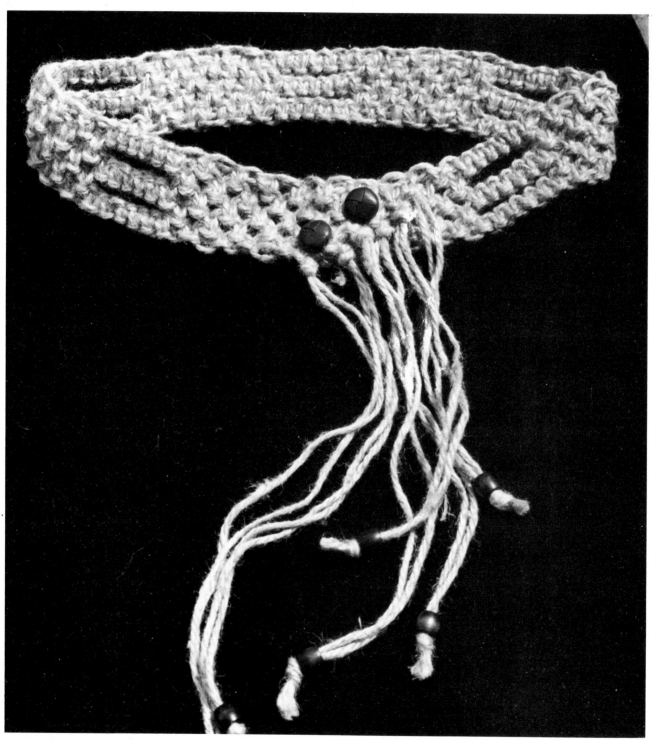

26. The belt above is an excellent example of using simple square knots to achieve an interesting effect.

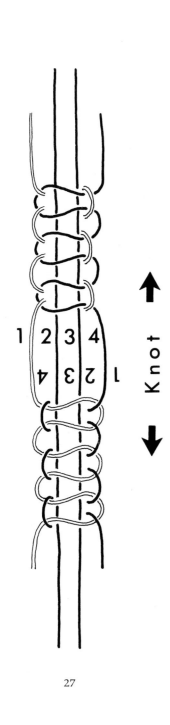

1 2 3 4

↑

K n o t

↓

27

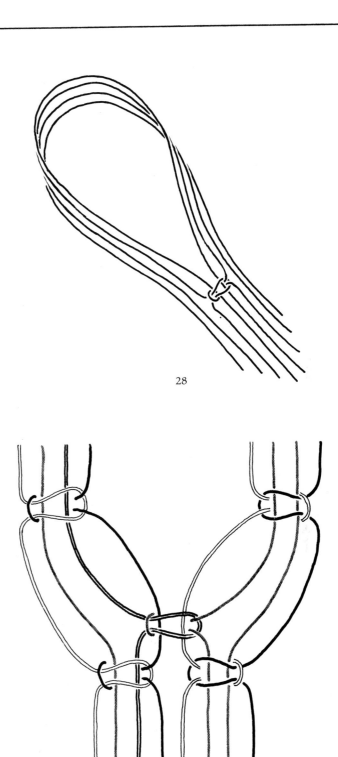

28

1 2 3 4 5 6 7 8

29

30. An attractive necklace ending that combines square knots, hitches, and beads.

square-knotted sennits of jute twine are set between areas of alternating square knots.

Cords. In designing your first project, you'll want to know how long to cut the cords. The answer is, naturally, "it depends." If your first project is to be a tightly knotted sennit, cut the core cords 6″ longer than the finished length desired, but cut the working cords 4 times as long, or even longer if the cord you've selected is very fine. If you're going to tie with all the strands, then all of them will need to be 3½ to 4 times the desired finished length. If you plan a lot of spaces with no knots, the cords can be cut shorter than if you plan to tie close. To understand this, cut four pieces of cord, each 12″ long. Pin them to your board and make a square knot sennit. Lay a ruler down beside it and see how long a piece you were able to knot before the ends got too short to use.

When choosing materials consider the function of the project you decide on. Feel the cord before you decide to buy it. If it feels scratchy it won't be comfortable as a necklace.

Start in the Center. The easiest way to make a sash or headband or strap of any sort, especially if any great length is involved, is to start in the middle (27). Work one way from the center to the end, however long you wish half of it to be. Then unpin your work and turn it around. Do the second half the same as you did the first. More ways will be discussed in the chapter on starting and finishing.

Slip-Over Necklace. This plan is equally elementary. Start in the center of the back and work both ways until you have enough length to slip over the head. Then bring the two incomplete ends around to the front so they lay alongside each other and pin them flat to the knotting surface. The back may stand on edge if there's any stiffness to what you've made. Join the two parts at the center front with a square knot in the alternate position, using two cords from the left-hand section and two from the right (28). From there on you can design whatever sort of an ending effect you wish (29). Your choice of material can make even the simplest plan an attractive accessory as shown by the necklace photograph (30).

Now you can see how easy it is to make a number of projects using only variations in half and square knot sennits and/or straps. Decide the spacing, number, and arrangement of knots in a cord you select, and design and make projects of your own.

2. Hitches

The half hitch is the second basic knot and it's even simpler than the square knot. Only two cords are involved, one working and one inactive, although the 4-strand sennit remains the unit of design most often used. The important thing in the half hitch is to *always keep the inactive element taut*. The working element does all the moving about to tie the knot.

The Half Hitch

To tie the half hitch, hold the inactive cord straight down and taut. Bring the working cord across in front, then around behind the inactive cord and out above the working cord, toward you (31).

To position the hitch, lift up the working cord end, pull the working loop up the taut inactive cord to wherever you want it, then let the cord end drop down (32).

You can hitch the right-hand cord working around the left inactive cord as well as the left-hand cord working around the right inactive cord.

Spiral Effect and Popcorn Sennit. Repeating left or right half hitches around a single cord creates a spiral effect. Alternating the working cord from the right-hand position to the left creates a totally different effect called the "popcorn" sennit (33) seen in the detail shown (34). Just make sure you always pull the inactive cord taut while knotting with the working one.

Using a pair of cords for each element, the same knotting sequence can produce a very effective flat sennit (35), sufficient in itself if done in a rather heavy cord, or it may be appliquéd as a fashion trim if worked in a more delicate cording.

To maintain the attractive flat look, it's necessary to keep the paired cords in order and laying flat alongside each other. The alternating half hitch isn't a good choice when any weight is to be suspended as the flatness tends to deform under such stress. A sennit where the core cords run straight through is a better selection under those conditions.

Sennit Variations. A number of attractive variations can be made with only four strands and the half hitch. You can half hitch with a single cord around the other three, here with #1 around #2, #3, and #4 (36). If you keep on, it will spiral. If you alternate, it will lay fairly flat.

Consider #2 and #3 as the core cords and alternately half hitch around them with #1 and then with #4.

To put more accent on the hitching cord, you could hitch a number of times before alternating, say 6 times with #1 around #2 and #3, then 6 times with #4

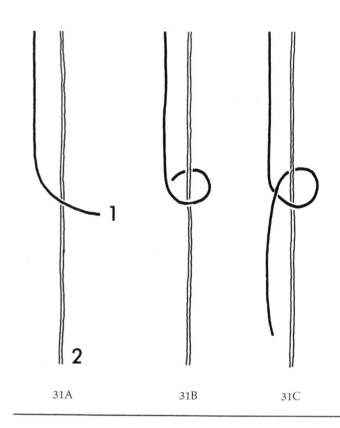

31A   31B   31C

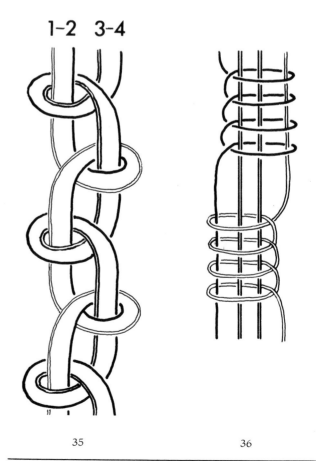

35   36

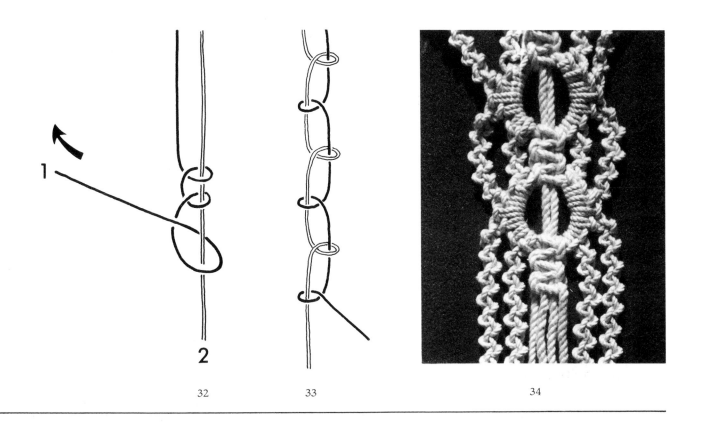

32   33   34

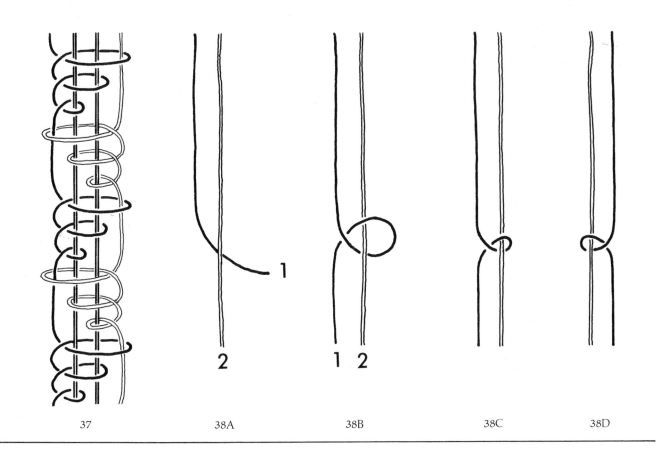

37   38A   38B   38C   38D

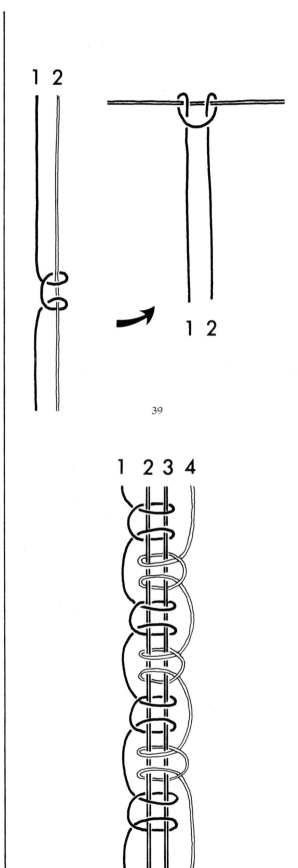

39

40

around #3 and #2. Pulling a bit tighter gives a wave effect.

Another variation can be alternating groups of three hitches of various sizes (37). Half hitch with #1 around #2, #3, and #4, then around only #2 and #3, and finally around only #2. Alternate the same way, hitching with #4 around #3, #2, and #1, then around #3 and #2, and finally around #3 only.

You can work out many inventions of your own using only half hitches and varying the order of knots as well as the number of strands used.

Reverse Half Hitch. Once you've learned the half hitch try the reverse half hitch. This is tied by carrying the working cord *behind* the inactive one, around it, and through, going away from you (38). Of course, there's a left hand and a right hand concept to be understood here too. Also, the same sennits just done in half hitches can be done in reverse half hitches.

The Lark's Head

Let's see what happens when you alternate a half hitch with a reverse half hitch. When tied on a vertical cord, it's usually referred to as a DRHH, meaning a double reversed half hitch.

Swung up into horizontal position, the double reversed half hitch takes on another name, "The Lark's Head Knot," and can be used for attaching cords to a holding or starting line (39). Either way, vertical or horizontal, from here on throughout the text this knot will be called a lark's head.

Lark's Head Sennits. Now let's explore some of the ways to use the lark's head on or with vertical core cords in the familiar 4-strand sennit. The most obvious way is to alternate lark's heads.

Tie a lark's head with #1 over core cords #2 and #3, alternating with a lark's head using #4 over the core cords #2 and #3 (40).

You can also vary the lark's head with half hitches and reversed half hitches (41). The simplest would be to half hitch with #1 over #2 and #3, lark's head with #1 over #2 and #3, and reverse half hitch with #1 over #2 and #3. Alternate in the same sequence using the #4 cord as the working cord.

Exchanging Cords. Another thing that's interesting to do with lark's heads is to exchange or cross over from one core cord or sennit to another. The first example (42) is useful to "lace up" two edges of adjoining sections. The other two 8- and 12-strand sennits (43, 44) make good men's belts, stiff and sturdy if worked in cotton seine cord. The core cords should be only a few inches more than the finished length, but the other cords require a working length of over 5 times the finished length. When you try a sample you'll find that lark's heads use up a lot of string.

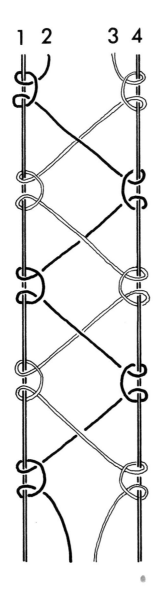

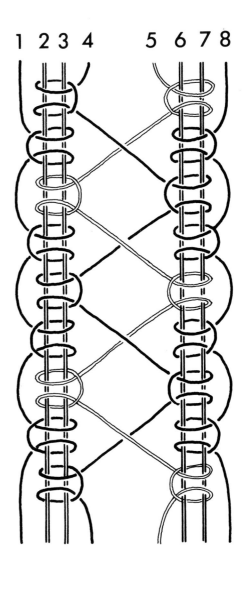

41

42

43

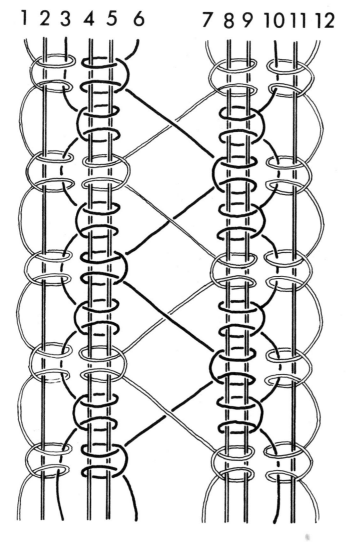

44

45

To make the 4-strand sennit, lark's head with #2 around #1 and with #3 around #4. Cross and lark's head with #3 around #1 and #2 around #4 (42). Cross again and repeat, alternating on down the sennit. It looks better if you make all the diagonal crossings overlap in the same pattern each time.

The 8- and 12-strand sennits shown incorporate the first sennit and expand by adding lark's heads to the sides. It's a lot easier to show in the diagrams (43 and 44) than to explain cord by cord.

Combining Knots

Square knots can be combined with half hitches very easily, as shown in the sennit diagramed (45), where alternating right and left square knots separate a repeated lark's head motif. This requires a square knot to the right, with #1 and #4 over the core cords #2 and #3, followed by two lark's heads, tying #1 over #2 and #4 over #3. Then make a square knot to the left with #4 and #1 over the core cords #3 and #2, followed by the lark's heads, #1 over #2 and #4 over #3 (45). Repeat the pattern. This sennit is easily expanded to an 8-strand strap. The necklace detail shown (46) is a good example of how this sennit can be used.

Another simple variation can be accomplished with additional half hitches and reverse half hitches flanking the central lark's heads but going over three strands each (47).

In a nylon braid or another slightly stiff cord, any of these variations should suggest a number of good necklace ideas. Just start at the center back and work until both sides measure about 14". Pin and number to bring all the strands in line and work out a medallion-type bib using lark's heads and square knots (47).

The Clove Hitch

The clove hitch is the other basic hitch variation. It's often called the double half hitch and the result is sometimes referred to as a "bar," usually qualified as being a vertical, horizontal, or diagonal bar, an "X," or a diamond. Whatever you want to call it, there are only two really vital variations: you can tie the knot to the right or to the left (48).

It's extremely important to remember that the inactive element of the clove hitch *must be held taut* in the direction you want the row of clove hitches to go.

Tying the knot looks a lot more complicated than it is. Remember that a clove hitch is really composed of simple half hitches—two for each clove hitch.

Clove Hitch to the Left or Right. Pin the inactive cord at the right to clove hitch to the left and hold it taut left in front of all the active cords you wish to clove hitch. The inactive cord may be the first or last of a given group of knot-

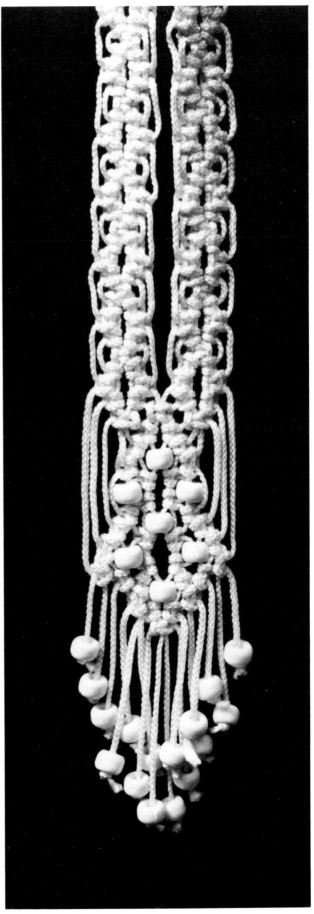

46

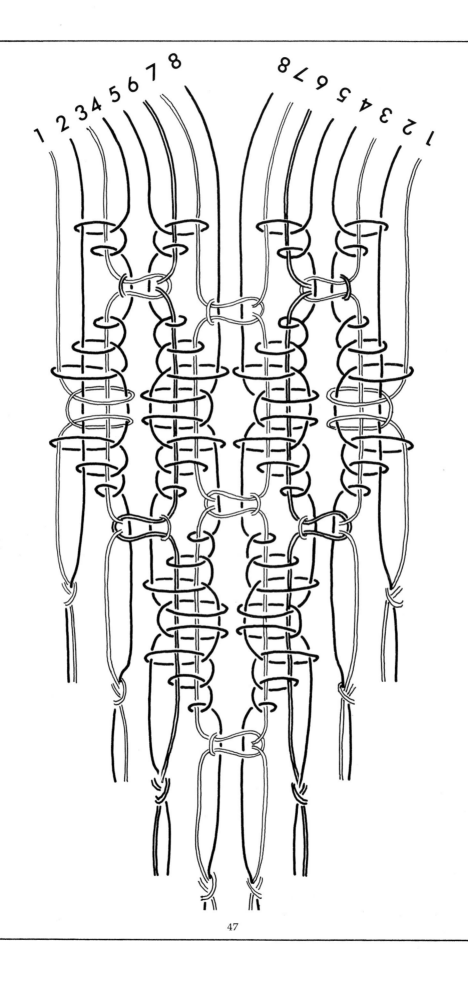

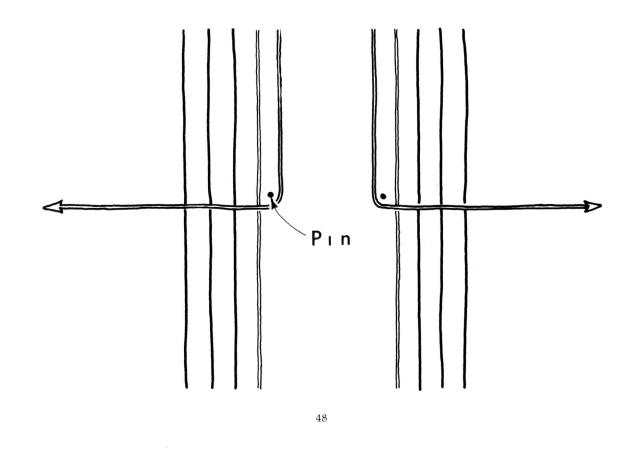

48

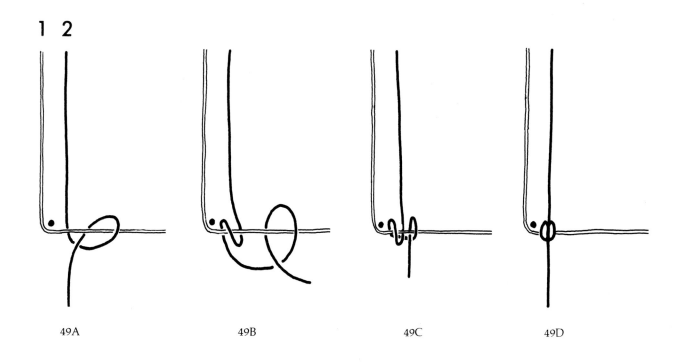

1 2

49A   49B   49C   49D

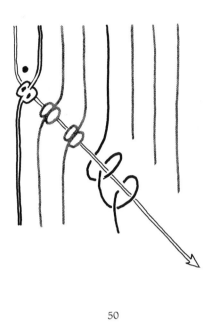

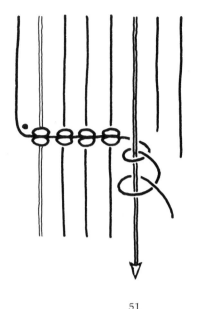

50

51

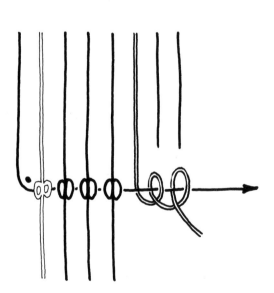

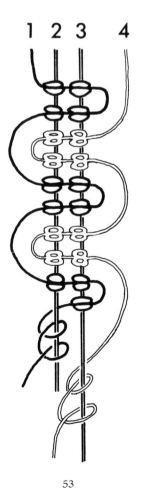

1 2 3 4

52

53

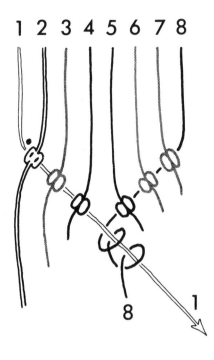

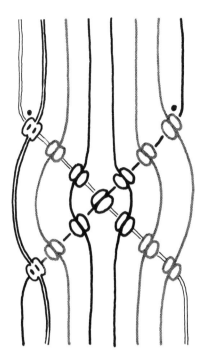

55A   55B

ting cords or it may be an entirely separate cord introduced only to carry the clove hitches. To clove hitch to the right, pin the inactive cord at the left (48). Bring the first active cord up, over, and down behind the inactive cord for one half hitch. Repeat the same thing with the same cord to complete the clove hitch (49). The first hitch usually falls about as shown in diagram B. When you see how the clove hitch is made, you'll learn to tighten the first half hitch before making the second half.

Variations of Clove Hitch Positioning. Diagonal (50), vertical (51), along a horizontal (52), or over the two core cords of the typical 4-strand sennit (53), the row of clove hitches will fall wherever you tighten them on the inactive cord.

You can make the rows go in waves if you hitch and hold in a wavy row. You can gather in and clove hitch around more than one holding cord if that suits your design, as was done in the wall hanging shown (54).

To make an "X," simply treat the first holding cord as another knotting cord when you encounter it, bringing the second leg of the "X" to the center (55). Repeats of this, with a square knot center, are the mainstay of the man's belt shown (56).

Different authors give different names to the many effects that can be achieved through using the clove hitch in series. A few of the most common might include: chevron or inverted chevron (57), zigzag (58), feather knot (59), and angling (60).

Try variations on diagonal clove hitching in 6- and 8-strand straps for many interesting ideas for belts, bag handles (61), or straps.

The boy's belt (62) is the next logical step—combining clove hitches with square knots. Later you'll see a number of examples where the clove-hitched line accents an area of alternating square knot fabric.

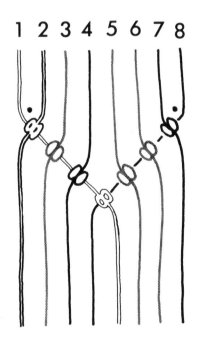

57

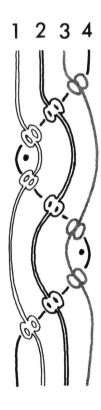

58

59

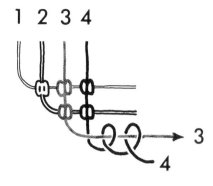

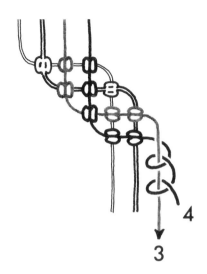

60A

60B

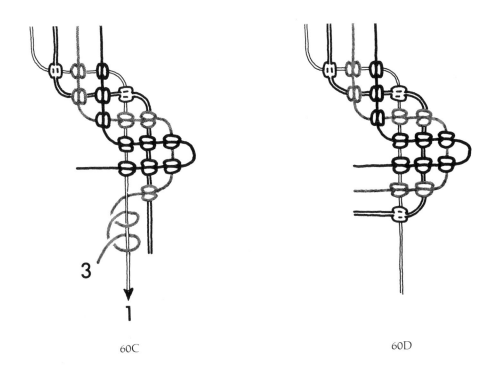

60C

3

1

60D

62

3. Fabrics

If you limit your knotting to sashes and neckpieces, you can get by without being too concerned with making wide pieces of macramé. But the time will come when you'll need a larger, repeatable textured or patterned area, solid or lightly filled, dense or transparent—a *fabric* of knots. Macramé fabrics by the yard are not the aim, but you'll find a fabric necessary when you start making "things," like bags, vests, seats, mats, or wall hangings.

It's impossible to catalog all the textures and patterns that can be made with macramé knots and their combinations. Organizing the various systems of developing fabrics, however, will help you understand how different fabrics are built. There are many approaches you can take to arrive at either an interesting simple texture, or a more involved, repeated motif. Both extremes are considered, arbitrarily perhaps, "fabrics."

Alternating Square Knot Fabrics

In Chapter 1 you saw how to join square knot sennits into square-knotted straps using a square knot in the alternate position. Now we'll go one step further to make fabrics of square knots. All the variations made in square-knotted straps can be expanded into fabrics. It becomes apparent that alternating square knots can go right around in a circle to make a tubular fabric when that's desired (and it will be when you make specific items based on that principle.) Note also that square knots, tied firmly in an alternating pattern, can end nicely on a 45° diagonal (63). Just remember to use a multiple of four strands when setting up the top row.

Lark's Head Edging. When you want the edges of an alternately square-knotted fabric to be a bit firmer, try tying a lark's head with the #1 cord around #2 and the last #3 around the #4 cord (assuming right-handed square knots) (64). This gives a slightly heavier look to the edge than you get by allowing the two cords to float when they have no alternate to tie with.

Spacing. Spacing is even more important in a fabric than in a strap. Leaving a lot of space between your alternating square knots yields an expandable, flexible fabric (65). The individual knots are tied in exactly the same way, but the length of cord left between them is regulated by judicial pinning or by eye. Don't think that pinning the square knot positions out horizontally guarantees the fabric will stay that wide. The weight of the cords will pull the whole thing down—a fact that works for you when you want a fabric to fit tightly around something.

Reversing Direction. The differences between square-

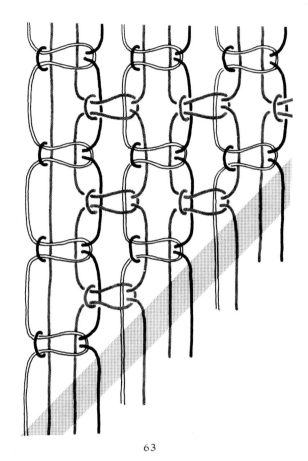

63

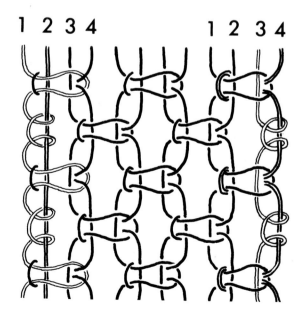

64

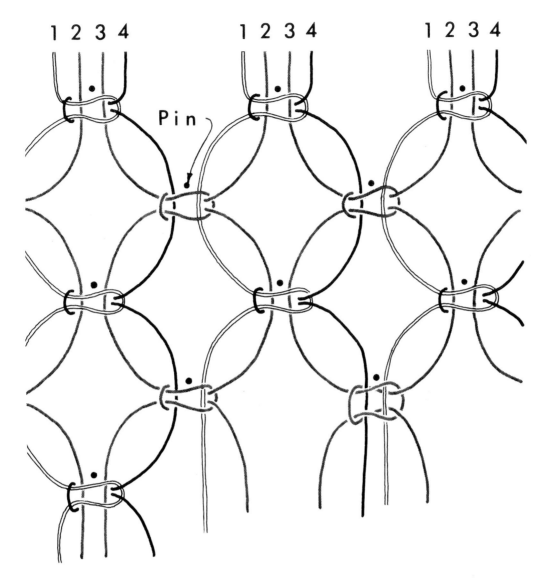

1 2 3 4   1 2 3 4   1 2 3 4

Pin

65

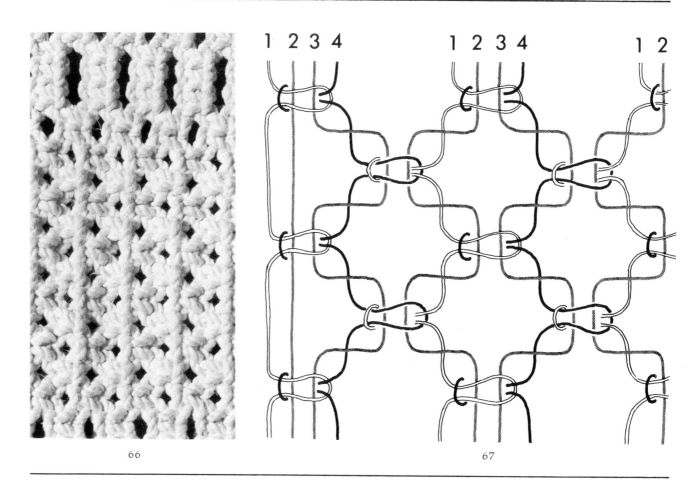

66

67

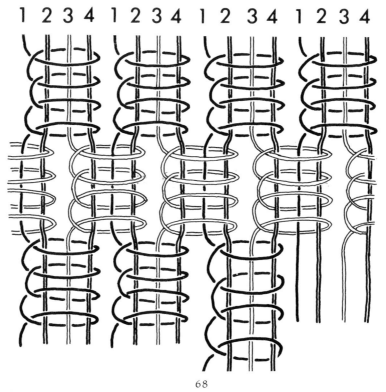

68

knotted sennits and fabrics come about because of the greater repetition of knots. For example, when the direction of the square-knotting is reversed in each alternating row in a fabric of any width, the ribbed effect that develops where the nubbins align becomes more apparent than when you have only 12 strands to work with (66).

Exchanging Cords. Exchanging the core cords in a spaced pattern gives another interesting effect in a fabric and makes it quite stretchy (67). Again, the core cords should always be exchanged in a consistent manner. The same knotting arrangement worked in two colors takes on a different appearance.

Any of the square-knotted sennits can replace the individual square knots in a fabric just as long as the concept of the alternating square knot is maintained. You could use two square knots each time, three knots, an echoing square knot, or a half knot spiral. Any of these might be repeated or you could vary your selection for each row.

Alternating Hitches

Most of the half hitched and lark's head sennits can be used in an alternating-position repeat too (68). For example, half hitch #1 around #2, #3, and #4; lark's head with #1 around #2, #3, and #4; reverse half hitch with #1 around #2, #3, and #4. Repeat this for each group of four cords. In the next row, hitch with #3 around #4, #1, and #2 of the next group; lark's head with #3 around #4, #1, and #2; reverse half hitch with #3 around #4, #1, and #2. The third row is the same as the first. Try this with any of the other hitched sennits for some interesting results.

In the mantel hanging shown (69), you'll see a half-hitched twill at the top, square knot sennits, and a row of double crosses, all joined together by horizontal bars of clove hitching and the alternating diamond with a square knot center at the bottom. It was done about 1910 in linen thread and shows there's nothing new about macramé!

69

70

71

Linear Hitches

A single row of clove hitching easily becomes an element of linear design: a horizontal clove-hitched cord might be straight, wavy, or zigzag. It could be one or more horizontal cords, perhaps of a heavier weight, introduced to tie together vertical sennits, or straps of various designs, but generally all of the same length. Next to alternating square knots, this is probably the method most often used in making fabrics. (70).

Naturally, designs aren't limited to the horizontal line. One very simple example is crossed diagonals. By paying attention to the intersection, you can maintain the appearance of a woven framework. This idea can be worked with two or more parallel lines of clove hitching or combined with areas in another pattern such as in the piece shown (71).

Many other linear patterns can make very pleasant fabrics. A typical one (72), consists of two parallel bars of clove hitching. The same order prevails in the leaf pattern (73), but here the lines are shaped to suggest leaves. Many of the clove-hitched strap designs are an open invitation to fabric development. Experiment a bit with units on the 45° diagonal, joining each row as it meets the adjacent one or joining each X only at the center. Open designs like these make good stole fabrics and can be worked as non-repeating elements for wall hangings. When you work with more than one color you'll need to watch the ever-changing place each color reappears (74). Proper plotting, however, will get a particular color to surface where you want it.

Chevrons, X's, and triple X's mix with square knots in the sampler shown. Note that you can take a small group of floating cords and simply reverse the order at intervals without tying any knots. These fabrics work up quite quickly, but are better in some cords than others. Like all macramé designs, its use must be tempered with good sense.

Solid Clove Hitches. Another obvious fabric is made with solid clove hitches. You can clove hitch on a series of horizontal lines or clove hitch the horizontal cord around the vertical ones (this takes an extremely long horizontal cord). Working with the vertical cords in one color and the horizontal cord in a contrasting one produces involved designs that can be predetermined by noting which cord does the hitching. The one that hitches will show, the cord hitched over disappears inside the clove hitch. The diagram (75) shows a simple Greek key. The photograph is of a black and white belt in a floral pattern, worked entirely in clove hitches (76).

You can work a solid area on diagonal cords, hitching one, two, or multiple colors for a range of other effects. A checkerboard or basketweave pattern is one possibility. Here you would most likely arrange your working cords by simply alternating the two colors. You might even decide you like the back side of clove hitching better than the front (77).

1 2 3 4 5 6 7 8 1 2 3 4 5 6 7 8 1 2 3 4 5 6 7 8

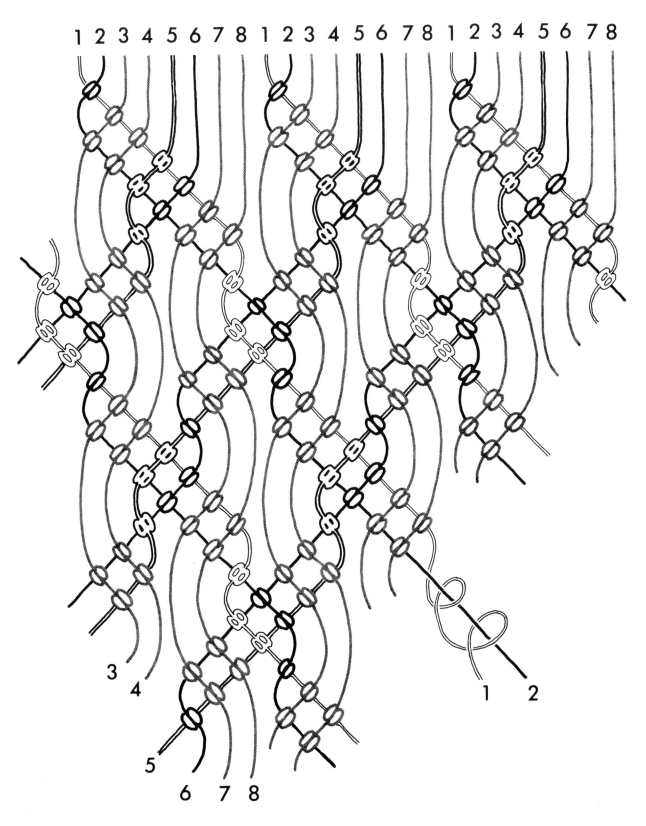

3

4

1 2

5

6 7 8

72

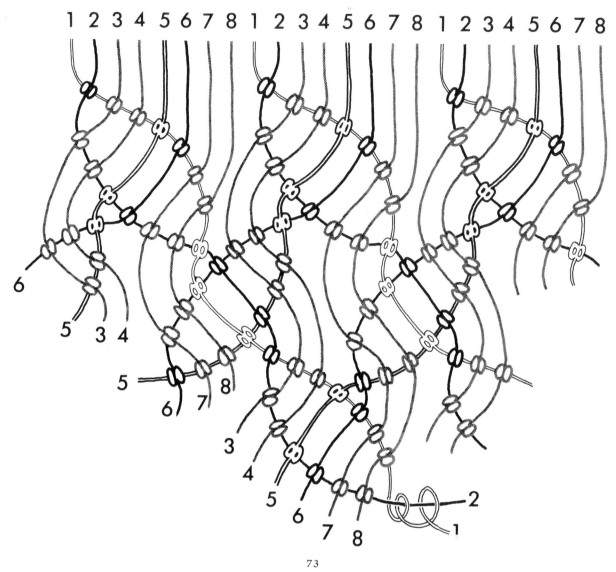

1 2 3 4 5 6 7 8 1 2 3 4 5 6 7 8 1 2 3 4 5 6 7 8

73

74

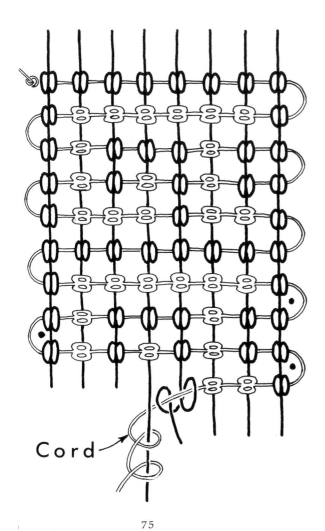

Cord

75

76

77

Repeats

Many motifs used in sennits can be translated into half-drop repeats and used as fabric designs. Actually that is the same principle as the alternating square knot positioning, a common form of repeat in textile prints. The diagram explains what happens (78).

In the second diagram, the gray diamond shape indicates the true repeat unit (79). The double diamond alone could be repeated, a different knot selected for the center, or the square knot used but not reversed for the alternating row (80). Most of the strap patterns developed can be worked into a fabric in this manner.

Lacings and Crossings.

Most of the patterns, with the exception of those based on the spaced alternating square knot, stay pretty much where they are knotted. For fabrics where some movement is desired, you might consider this approach: simply lace up straps as you would a shoe to form a larger whole.

Crossings can also be used in combination with the lark's head (81). Actually this method could be used with any sennit, but it's particularly effective in designs that include other lark's head knots.

Exchanging Working Cords. In a series of square-knotted sennits for instance, take one working cord from sennit A and one from sennit C and tie the next square knot over the core cords of sennit B, then return the working cords to their original sennit (82). All the sennits must work in unison on this one.

Interlocking. Some knots and their variations can be interlocked with pleasing results. In adjacent sennits of the butterfly knot the working cords can simply be intertwined without knotting them to the next sennit (83). This will work on some of the clove-hitched sennit braids too. You'll want to experiment with these ideas when you want a looser fabric but single sennits might get out of hand. This method works best when the sennits are allowed to hang freely. The interlocking feature should limit the movement rather than take weight. In other words, this system makes good skirts and curtains, but not stool seats or doormats.

The Overhand Knot. Even the overhand knot can be used for fabrics. One form, popular in nautical work and often used for filling in areas, is the marlin knot, an overhand knot tied around another cord at right angles to the first. Other even simpler forms, often used for fringed borders, are done with the overhand knot either in pairs of cords or tied with one cord around the other. Either way it results in a netting-like construction (84).

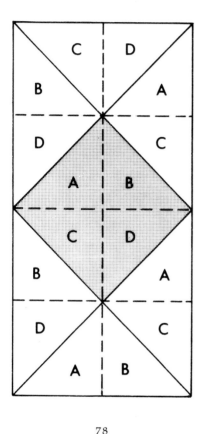

78

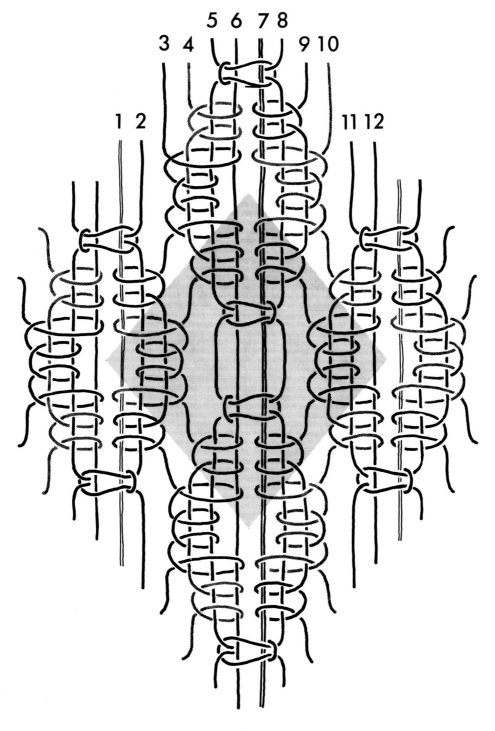

79

1 2 3 4 5 6 7 8 1 2 3 4 5 6 7 8

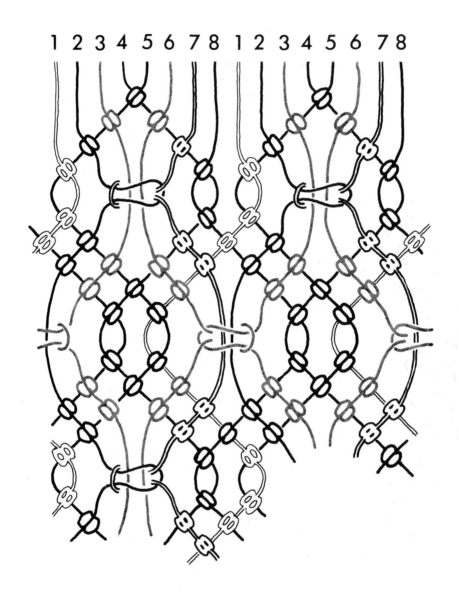

80

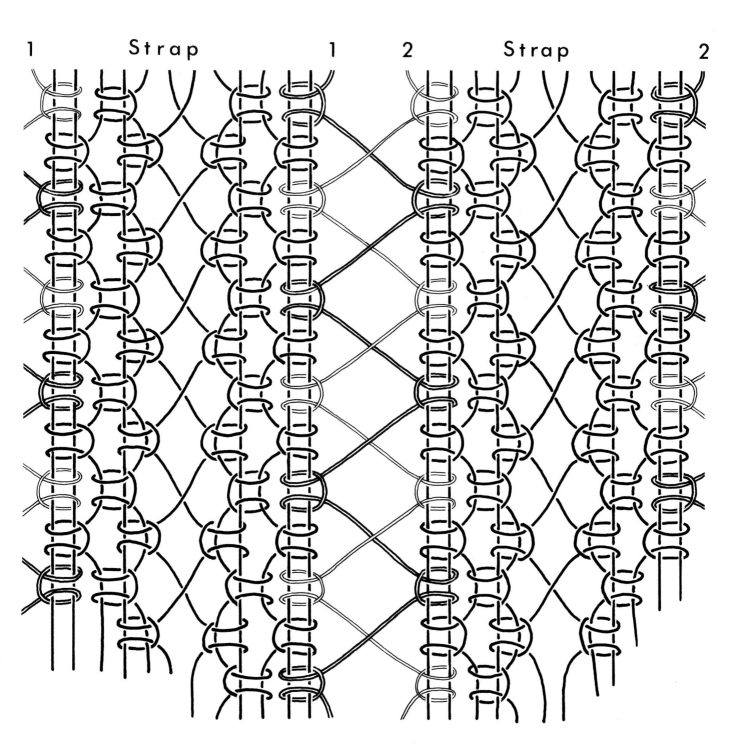

81

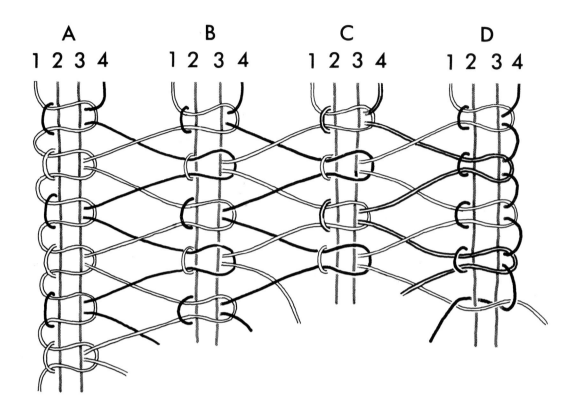

A   B   C   D
1 2 3 4   1 2 3 4   1 2 3 4   1 2 3 4

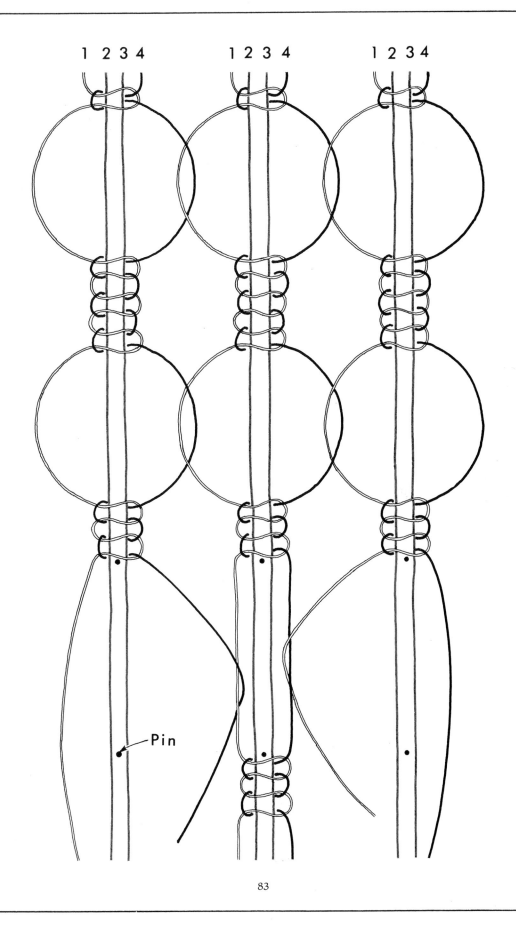

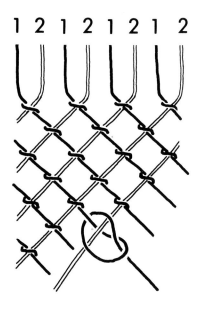

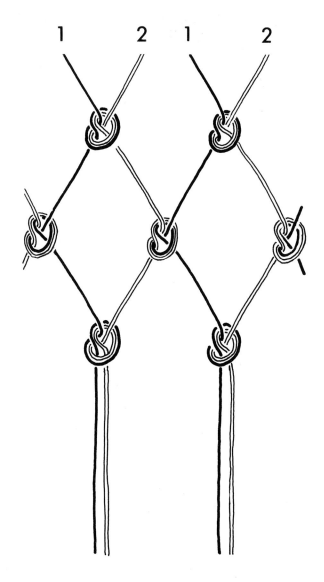

84A

84B

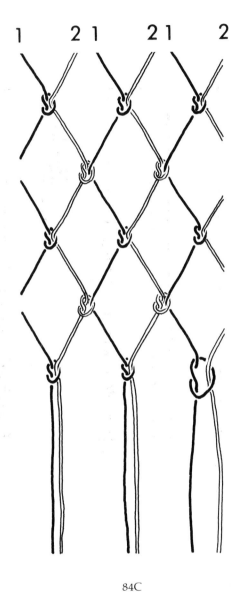

1   2 1   2 1   2

84C

Fabric Development.

You'll find the use of graph paper a particular advantage in developing repeat-design fabrics. It's simply a matter of counting squares to arrange pins at regular intervals for spacing the knots. Diagonals can be pinned accurately from corner to corner and working symmetrically becomes almost automatic.

Try some fabric swatches as experiments. Pin on 16, 24, 32, or 48, or many more cords, and plan a fabric. With the overhand knot you can fringe both ends of a seat mat or a stole. With a change of cord you can work up a set of table mats. As you'll see when we reach the chapter on making "things," the rectangle with the fringe at both ends is the basis of several projects. It may be boring, but it's certainly a good idea to record the type, name, and cost of the cord used in such samples along with a note about the length you cut to start with. It comes in handy when planning future projects.

4. Beginning and Ending

So far the starting method has been to pin cords to a knotting board and work from the center to each of the ends. There was no problem understanding cord length because the cut length *is* the working length when you work this way. But often it's necessary to begin from a starting line at the top, and then the working length of a cord is measured from the starting line to the end of the cord. The length of the cords you fold in half must, therefore, be cut double that. So now we'll have three terms to contend with (85): the cut length which is two times the working length; the working length which is 3½ or 4 or more times the desired finished length; the finished length, usually given for the actual length knotted. Any allowance for fringe or tassel is noted separately and added to the working cord length, or doubled and added to the cut length.

The Holding Cord

There are a lot of ways to commence working from a starting line. One is to have your starting line be a cord. Cut it a bit longer than you want the width of the finished piece to be. Then tie an overhand knot in each end and pin through the knots to the knotting board, stretching the starting line taut. The simplest way to attach the cords is to let half the cord fall behind the starting line, the other half in front, then start knotting (86). It's so simple, however, that it has one disadvantage—the loops slip until you get the first knot tied unless you hold the core cords securely with a pin. You can do exactly the same thing if you start from a dowel, a stick, a ring, or a hole punched in another material.

Attaching the Working Cords

The most common method of attaching the working cords is the lark's head. It's simple enough—a half hitch followed by a reverse half hitch with both ends left free. To form the lark's head on a cord, or any other type of starting line, first fold the cut lengths in half at the center. Next push the fold down from the top, behind the starting line. Reach up through the loop and pull the working ends down and through the loop, then tighten the lark's head (87).

It's often suggested that a row of clove hitches immediately follow below the lark's heads. This can be done by introducing a new cord, or you can use the first working

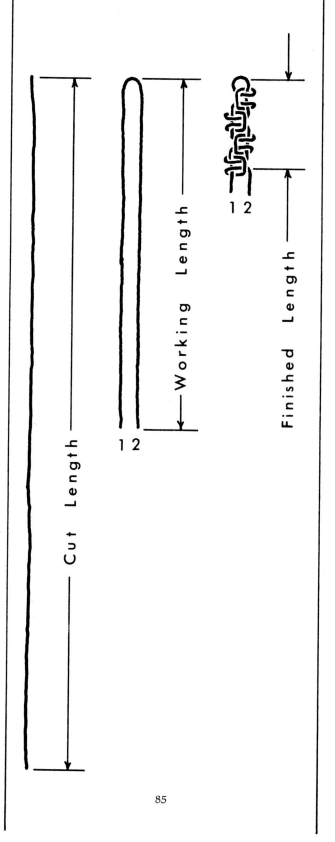

Cut Length

1 2

Working Length

1 2

Finished Length

85

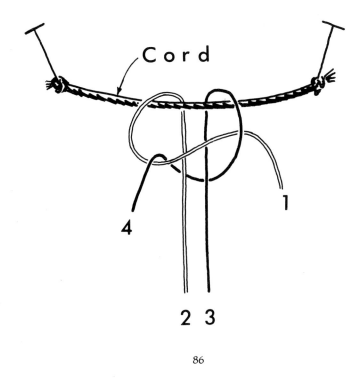

Cord

4

1

2 3

86

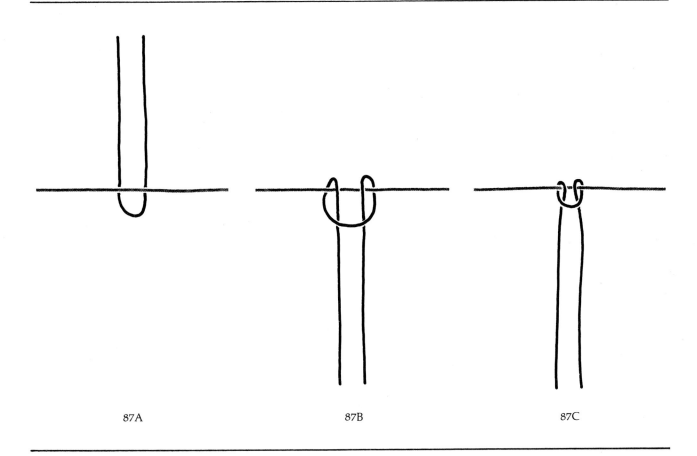

87A   87B   87C

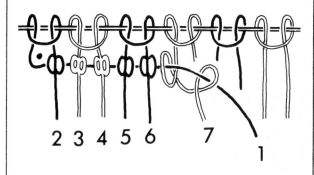

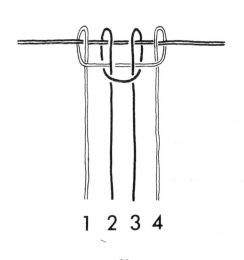

2 3 4 5 6 7 1

88

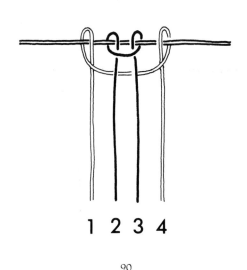

1 2 3 4

89

1 2 3 4

90

cord just mounted. This procedure evenly sets the spacing, because it positions the lark's heads equally along the starting line (88). Its disadvantage is in its appearance, particularly if you want to accent the 4-cord grouping.

4-Cord Groupings. If you do wish to accent the 4-cord grouping, consider a lark's head over a lark's head. Tie a lark's head on the starting line as before. Spread it apart enough to tie on a lark's head inside the first one, over both the tie cord of the first knot and the starting cord (89). You can vary this by tying on the first knot, spreading it, and setting the center knot of each group on top of the outside one (90). In any one piece, it's probably best to choose one way or the other.

Sennit Starting Line. You can also use a sennit as the starting line. The one-winged butterfly is one possibility if you want a series of evenly spaced loops (91). The lark's head chain variations can also be used as belt straps for starting a skirt or apron.

One big advantage in using any sennit is having a simple way of working out the exact spacing you want between working cords. The length of horizontal strap between them controls the spacing.

Doubled Cord. It's often possible to use a doubled cord as a starting line, and sometimes that's improved by using an additional cord to make lark's heads in between the Attached working cords (92). The ends of the additional cord can be knotted into the starting line or worked into the piece as two more working cords. This extra reinforcement is a particularly good idea where a single cord starting line might be subject to excessive strain—such as across the front of a purse opening, or along the neck back of a vest.

Shaped Startings

You can start round items with lark's heads, too. Form a loop of the same cord as you'll use to tie with, letting the ends overlap to working cord length. One lark's head over the double cord area nets one group of four. Add as many more groups as required. You could also use clove hitches or a fancy heading to make a pom-pom at the center of a hat. Lark's heads can be used to mount working cords on a shaped starting cord, too, provided the knotting within the shape reinforces it (93). If you use a paired cord as the starting line it can be brought into the body of the work as an additional group of four when it's no longer needed as a starting line. This is handy for the tip of a belt or the point of a purse flap.

Rings. Exploit plastic or metal rings, too, using lark's heads to attach cords so something can be hung off the ring. Or you can group the strands in any number of directions around the ring for starting round items such as the bottom of the bottle cover shown (94).

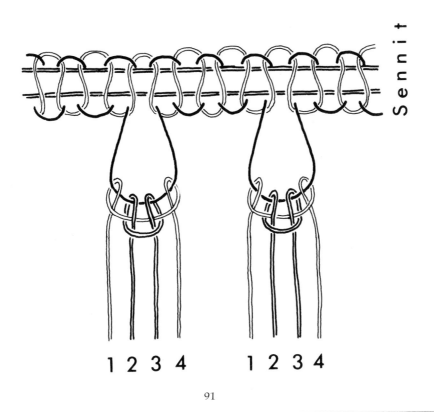

Sennit

1 2 3 4   1 2 3 4

91

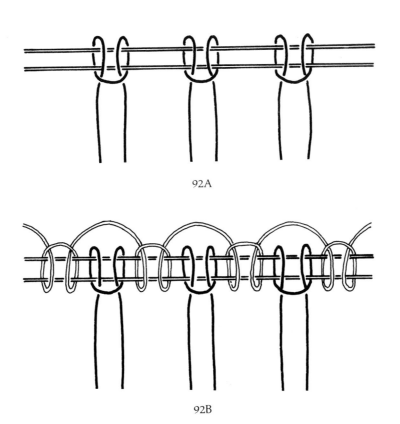

92A

92B

Or perhaps you'd like a covered ring for a drawstring top. This requires one long strand to form one working length, a reverse hitch (to complete the lark's head on that side), a series of lark's heads to cover the ring, and a last lark's head with the working cord left free. You would then use lark's heads to add the necessary number of working cords between these ends to provide the total number of working cords desired (95).

You can start from a loop by covering cord instead of a ring, but it will deform when weight is applied. Find the center of the cut lengths and do a chain of lark's heads, alternating or all with one cord around the other. Bring the ends together so a loop of the desired size is formed. The four strands become the cords for your sennit.

In fact, lark's heads can be used to enclose the adjacent working cords right around other working cords to provide as many groups of four working cords as you wish (96). This can be a useful technique for starting the bottom of a bottle (97).

Starting Without a Cord

It's also possible to start square knotting from nothing, though you'll need two pins temporarily. Set the pins far enough apart so that two cords can fit between them. Loop your cut lengths over the pins, letting the two center ends become the core cords of a 4-strand sennit, while the two outside lengths are the knotting cords (98). Then, start knotting.

When the sennit is long enough, or if you plan to exchange core cords with working cords, remove the pins and pull the core cords down so that the two loops at the top become tiny.

With a few more pins and the concept of the alternating square knot, this method can be enlarged. Place another cord over another pin on one side of the first sennit (cords #5 and #6), then add another cord on the other side (cords #7 and #8), down just far enough to place the knots in the alternating position comfortably below the first one tied (99).

Belt with Pointed End. This is one easy way to start a belt with a pointed end, if you've used a square knot base for the design. Just pull the loops in as you go and re-pin through the knots (100). Adding lark's heads as shown will make a sturdier belt.

Wall Hangings. Starting working cords in this manner is a useful way to begin many practical items. You can also start wall hangings this way. A simple loop added and drawn through the two top "ears" will give you a hanging ring. If you position the loop's knot so it falls behind the work, the appearance will be much neater.

Fasten-in-the-back Necklace. A variation of the square-knotted sennit starting from nothing is a good way to begin a fasten-in-the-back necklace (101). For the looped end, place one cut length folded in half over a pin and an-

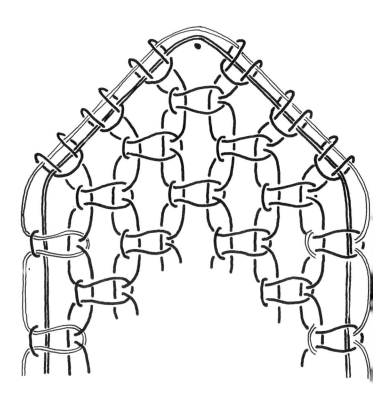

93

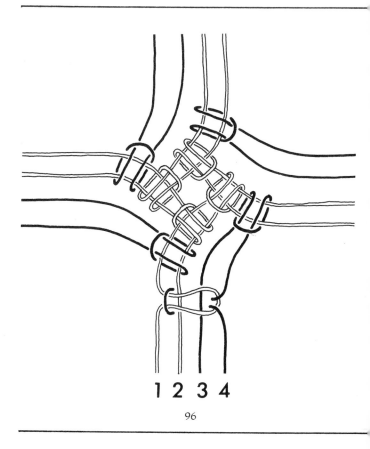

1 2 3 4

96

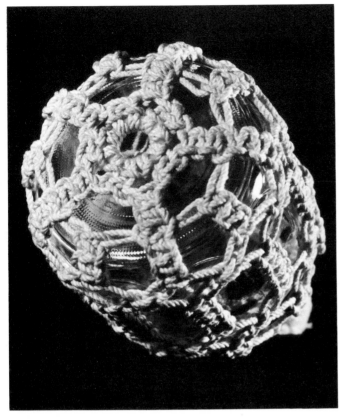

94

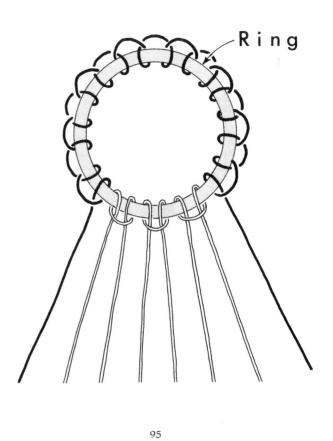

Ring

95

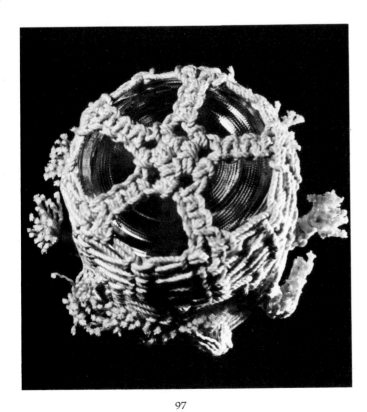

97

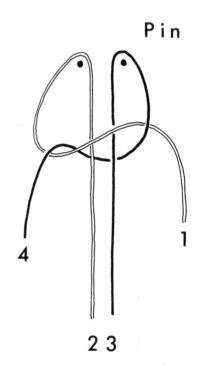

Pin

4

2 3

1

98

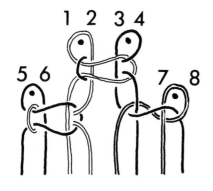

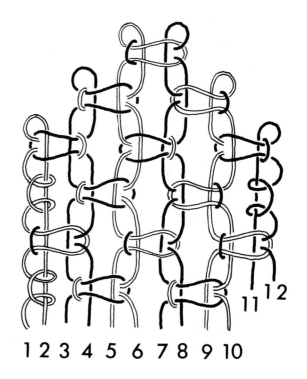

99

100

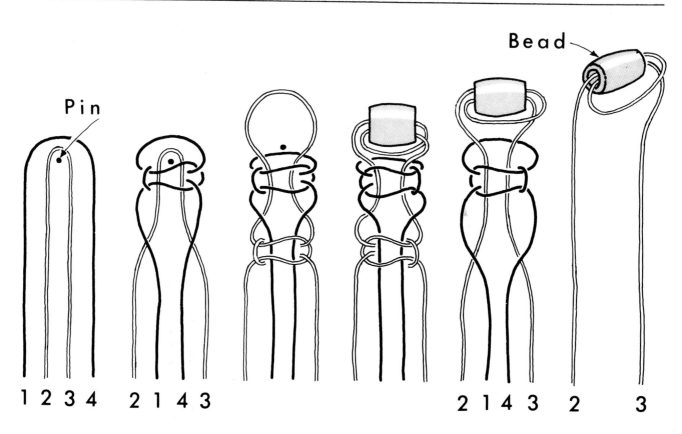

101

other length folded in half over the first length. Then tie one square knot and pull up a loop from the bend in the core cords. Exchange core cords and working cords and tie another square knot, adjusting the loop to the necessary size before tightening the second square knot. To begin the latch end, string a bead to the center of the core cord and run the strand through the bead a second time if possible. Pin out the working cords close to it and tie one square knot. Exchange core cords for working cords and tie a second square knot. When your two sennits are the length that you want they can be brought together in any number of attractive ways.

Bag with Handle. Starting square knotting from the middle of nowhere also applies to one style of bag with a built-in handle. You could consider it for a shoulder strap too. Gather as many cords as you will eventually want into a bundle and work a paired square-knotted sennit. Branch off by dividing the strands from either end of the "handle" bundle again and again until you have the groups of four cords each that you require to begin the body of the bag (102).

Decorative Edgings

Many wall hanging designs rely on a stiffener or at least a heavier horizontal than would be provided by a single cord. These designs often call for some macramé above the topmost horizontal as well. It could easily consist of a series of points constructed by square knotting from pins, either triangular or as a series of short sennits. Don't get carried away with decorative edgings, however, as they do tend to topple.

Picots. You're more apt to see a picot of sorts formed by extending the clove hitches that go around the starting line (103). The simplest picot, of course, is made by forming small arcs between the hitches. The same arc can be made with a knot in each loop. Or six working cords can form a triple picot as shown. And it could just as well be double or quadruple. You could also mix clove hitching and lark's head attachments in any arrangement. It's easy to see the possibilities of introducing color in a decorative heading, and this can get quite intricately involved. It's also possible to have a built-in hanger for your wall hanging. Any sennit capable of carrying the weight can be attached with clove hitches to a rigid starting line by clove hitching the ends as shown (104).

Starting from a Point. Clove hitching can also be used to start a piece from a point (105). Lay down the center length, folded in half. Pin that and lay the length that will be the flanking working cords centered across it. Make two horizontal clove hitches with center cord around the cross one, that is with cord #1 around #2, as at B. Continue to lay on as many additonal cords as are required to provide the number of working cords desired. A shaped

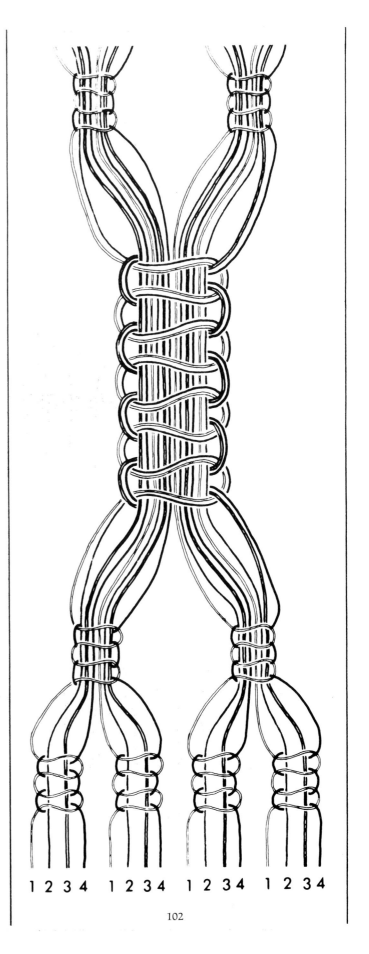

1 2 3 4   1 2 3 4   1 2 3 4   1 2 3 4

102

103A

103B

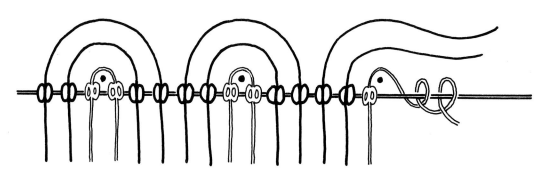

103C

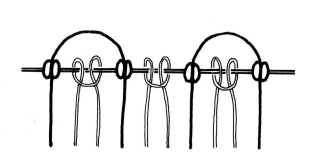

103D

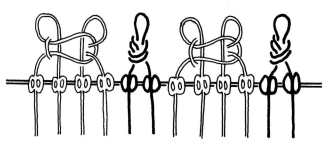

103E

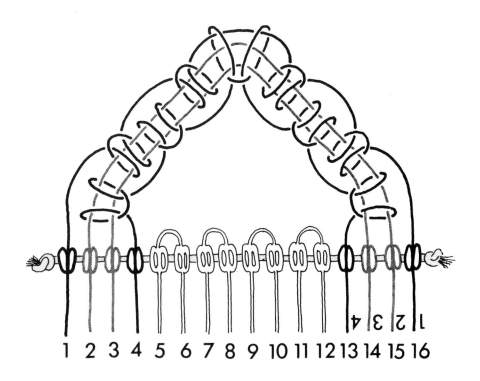

1 2 3 4 5 6 7 8 9 10 11 12 13 14 15 16

104

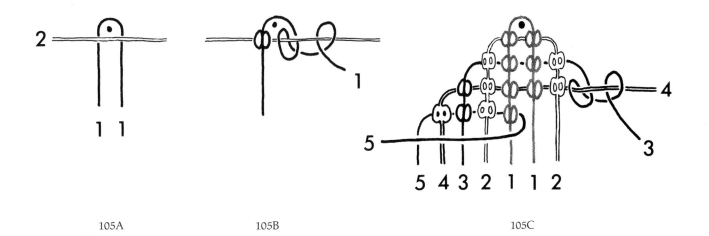

105A   105B   105C

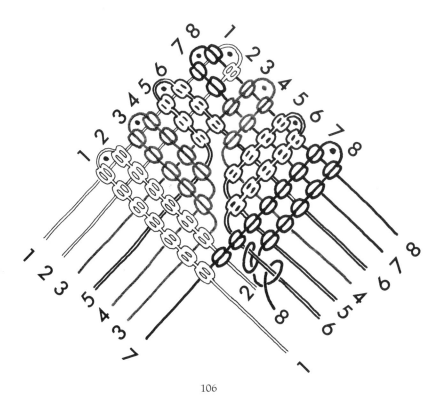

106

start can be developed in the same manner if you pin carefully.

Turned on the diagonal, it's also easy to work a buttonhole into clove hitching. Just turn back the added cord at the slot position and use the other end for the next row (106). Note the #5 cord in the previous diagram (105) to see how simply a buttonhole is formed in a horizontally clove-hitched point.

Rectangular Shapes

Starting rectangular shapes is one way clove hitching really shines. Compare the pointed buttonhole start (106) to this method (107). You simply let the cords run on through so you have working cords extending out from a solid center in four directions. This arrangement is ideal for the bottom of a bag or a box.

You might also start from interweaving, running through or doubling back as shown (108). You can also combine weaving and clove hitching as was done for the bottom of the bag (109). But let your imagination run free. There are many ways to start a piece of macramé. It would be a shame to cover up an interesting texture such as the dried cactus shown when you can start by just running the cords in and out of the holes (110). On a pre-punched or pre-drilled piece, where the holes are too small for a double cord, use a single one held by an over-hand knot, or run the cords in one hole and out another.

Finishing the Ends

Sooner or later you'll come to the end of your rope. You can cut off the ends evenly with scissors, a safety-edge razor blade, or a Hot Knife (manufactured by Weller). To cut straight, make sure you hold the cord at right angles to the cutting edge. If you use a razor blade and have a lot of cords to cut off to the same length, a metal straightedge is often a big help. Hold it down firmly on the cords and slide the razor blade along the edge.

Cutting. A Hot Knife will cut nylon cord very neatly, but it must be kept cleaned off with a damp rag so the melted plastic doesn't build up and discolor the cords you're cutting. Hold the cord you wish to cut flat on a hard surface and roll it towards the knife a bit as you make the cut. Let the heat of the knife do the cutting, rather than whacking through with the sharp edge. That way it seals the ends of the fibers against each other so they don't ravel.

Gluing. On fibers that don't melt, you can dip the ends into a solution of ½ white glue, ½ water. This works quite well and doesn't discolor or stain any but the most delicate cords. If you knot the end and dip only the knotted

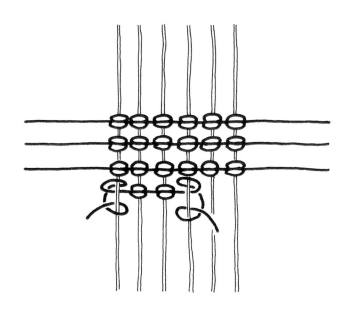

107

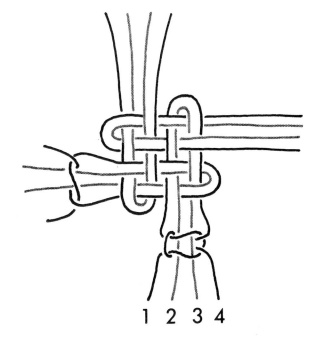

1 2 3 4

108

109

110

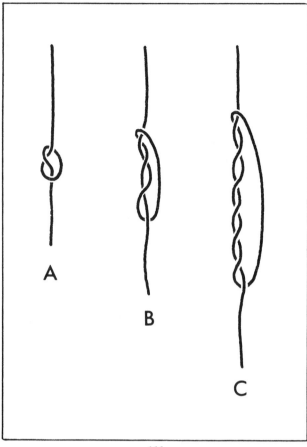

A

B

C

111

112

part neatly into the glue mix, the color change isn't very noticeable.

Knots. Suitable knots for the end of small strands include, of course, the simple overhand knot. You may like its appearance better if you add one twist as you tie it, or five or six twists to make a barrel knot (111).

Beads. Hiding the ends inside or behind something is another method of finishing the ends to be considered. You can string on a bead and glue the end inside the bead. Or knot just under the bead and wedge the knot up inside the bead. Then, for safety, add glue to the end before trimming. Certain shells can also be used, with the cord ends knotted inside. Or you could tie on a feather (112).

Wrapping. Another ending device is wrapping cord around each cord or around two or more cords (113 and 114). Lay the wrapping cord (or use one of the gathered strands as the wrapping cord) on top of the other cord or cords. Start at the bottom, letting the second turn go *over* the first turn to provide an "anchor" for turns above. After a few turns have been made, insert a blunt pointed needle so you won't penetrate any one cord later when you pull the end of the wrapping cord down through the wrapping to become part of the tassel or to be cut off. When you finish, thread the end through the needle's eye and get hold of the needle—with pliers if necessary—and pull the end through. If a needle large enough to take the cord is too large to pull through, insert a doubled wire instead.

Another way of wrapping, which is the way they do it in the Navy, is "whipping." For this, lay in a looped end first, wrap from the bottom up as before and insert the end through the loop formed in the beginning (115). Pull the loop down so that it's beneath the wrapping and you can cut off both ends. There's little danger of it coming undone if you've wrapped tightly enough to start with.

The idea of wrapping can also be used to gather a number of doubled strands together for a tassel, or for another way to introduce color, or to add textural interest into the body of macramé work (116).

Fringe. There are times when simplest is best. Knotting and fringing the ends of your cords by unraveling them is a case in point. If you have a twisted cord, untwist it and you'll see that each strand is itself twisted of smaller fibers. If desired, these too can be untwisted for a fluffier tassel effect. On braided cords, pick the fibers apart with a blunt needle. If it's a cord with a different color inside (117), slide the braided exterior sheath up the core a bit, exposing the material inside. Snip off the core, bring the sheath back down, and knot, ideally at the place the core ends. Then fringe only the sheath threads.

Incidentally, don't underestimate the power of steam. It will fluff out many fibers (braided polypropylene makes very nice fluffy ends) and will allow you to comb out the strands of most nylon cords so they'll hang straight. Steaming can often revive kinked-up cords that

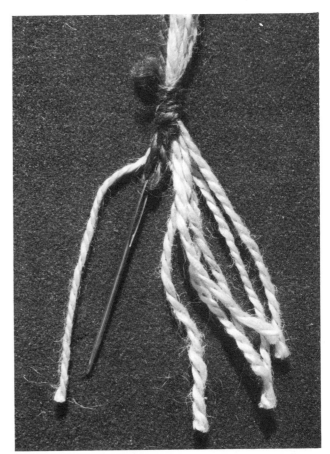

113

114

115

116

you've tied wrong and untied again, too, making them suitable to re-use.

Some pieces can be ended with a double row of clove hitches. The ends are then pulled up and over the intervening cords and tied in pairs on the underside.

Hiding the Ends. In finishing some cords a facing of twill tape can be used. Turn the macramé face down and machine stitch through the ends onto the tape. Then trim the ends so they fall beneath the tape. Fold it over and whip to the backside of the macramé.

You can, of course, rely on glue if a piece is not going to be washed vigorously (if it is, tie and sew first, then glue.) On nylon and other heat-affected synthetics, heat-fusing with an iron will seal a knot as well or better than white glue will. Use a piece of aluminum foil over the cords to keep any melted plastic off your iron. A match or lighter also works but discolors the cord.

All the directions that tell you to "bring ends to wrong side and finish off" really mean to take a few stitches with each cord, or if it is a twisted cord, untwist it and take a few stitches with each of the separate strands, then glue or knot and glue. If this is done so the stiches and the knots fall regularly between strands raised on the right side, it's usually not too obvious.

In any particular project, you may find ways of inventing the ideal solution for that project. If it's a wall hanging with papier-mâché beads in the body, you could embed the ends in papier-mâché. If it features wood you might design a wooden end-hiding device. What will happen to the ends has to be a major consideration when you design any piece of macramé.

117. Cord ends untwisted for a fluffed, finished effect (left), and unfinished cord ends showing the core cord still exposed (right).

5. Fancies

The other 5% of the knotting work in macramé consists of tassels, balls, braids, coxcombing, weavings, combinations, sennit braiding, and just plain tricky things. The supply of ideas in this area is seemingly endless. Combine knots you already know; investigate occupational sources, particularly seamen's work; look into the Orient; and don't neglect the Boy Scout Handbook.

It's difficult to present the vast assortment of "fancies" in an easy-to-more-difficult progression, as their differences are not necessarily in the amount of skill required (often surprisingly little) but in their dissimilarity. Unfortunately it's only possible to investigate a tiny portion of the huge number of variations.

Square-Knotted Fancies

The button loop is one very easy way of introducing surface interest in alternating square knot work. It's simply a sennit of square knotting looped back into itself (118).

It takes about five to seven knots to make a sennit long enough to loop back. The number will vary with the size of the cord being used. To begin the loop, leave a slight space below the last square knot tied with the selected 4-strand group. Tie a square knot sennit which is as long as the size loop you want. Separate the core cords from the working cords and bring the core cords forward, up, and above the first knot of the sennit just tied. Run them between the core cords and out below the button. Bring the working cords from the sennit in position to form the next square knot over the core cords (119).

There's no reason that a sennit lifted from its original position can't be crossed regularly or turned or looped over in any number of positions, providing enough of the alternating square knotting carries on to give body to the work. Experiment as you go along—the simple braiding of sennits comes out of this kind of thought. Two square-knotted sennits can be shaped to entwine with each other as they do at the sides of the hanging shown (120). And two half knot spirals can entwine in much the same way.

Clove-Hitched Variations

Lifting a section or adding a secondary strain works in tightly clove-hitched designs too. Although clove hitching isn't usually thought of as a sennit, flat areas of clove hitching can be made to intertwine with each other if it's plotted out first. As you saw in Chapter 2, angular shapes are easy to make. Take two and you can set them together.

Carry on extra set of cords along the back or within the holding cord and let it come free at regular intervals for a "finny fabric" look (121).

118

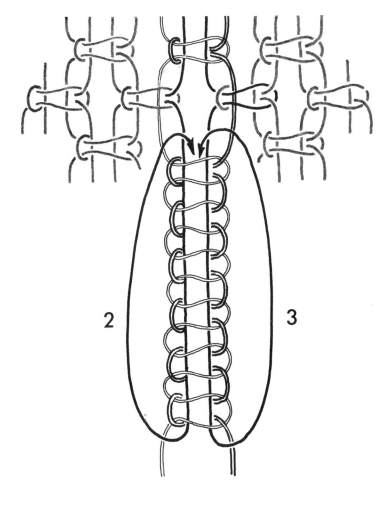

1 2 3 4

2   3

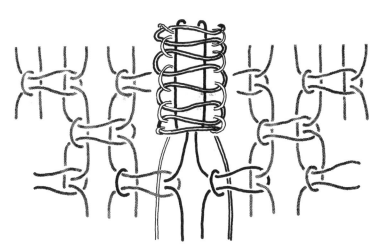

119

120

121

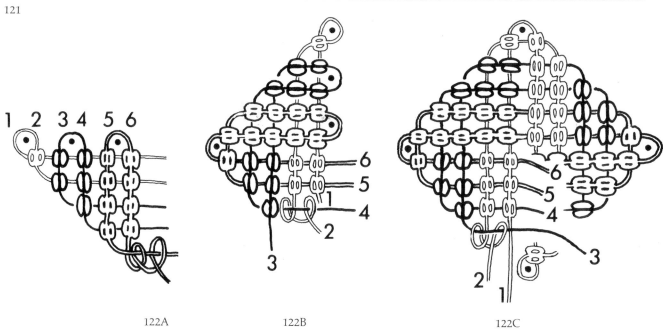

122A   122B   122C

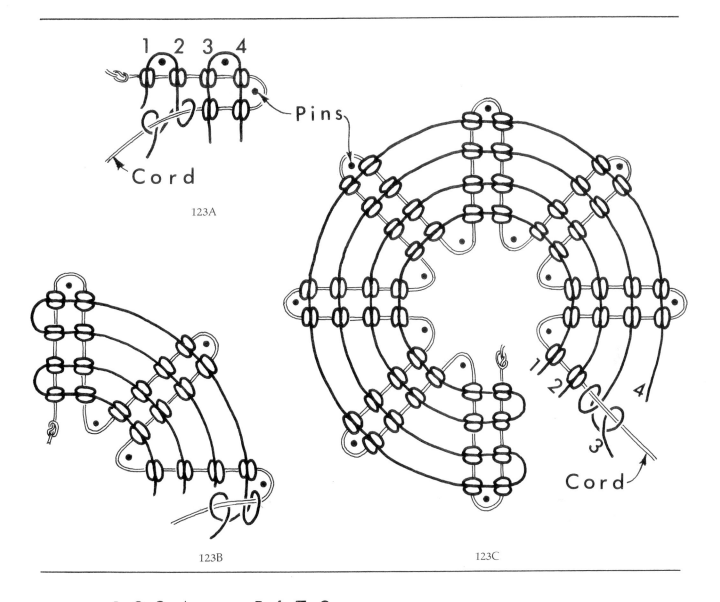

123A

123B

123C

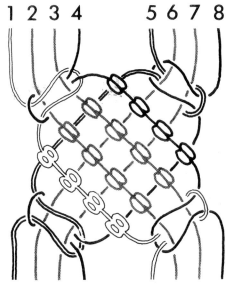

124

125

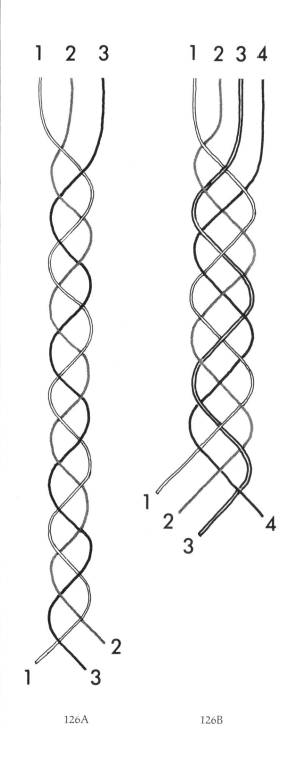

1 2 3

1 2 3 4

1
2
3 4

1
2 3

126A   126B

Angular Twisty. You'll find a couple of tricky things happen when you're fooling around with clove hitches. For an "angular twisty," the diagram shows six working cords but you could use any number. Start by clove hitching around #1 with #2, #3, #4, #5, and #6 in turn. Bring #2 across to the right and clove hitch around it with #3, #4, #5 and #6. Repeat with #3, #4, and #5 held across to the right and hitched about with the remaining cords each time. Now turn the whole triangular piece ¼ turn (as in B) and, considering the cords as they hang down vertically, do the exact same thing again. Make a ¼ turn and repeat, another ¼ turn and you're back where you started. Keep going in the same manner for a second layer, and you'll see that a sort of square accordion develops (122).

Circular Twisty. To make a "circular twisty" with an open look, use four working cords and a separate holding cord. Pin the holding cord down as before and clove hitch around it with #1, #2, #3, and #4 in turn. Place the second pin and bring the holding cord back to the left, clove hitching around it with #4, #3, #2, and #1 in turn. Depending on the diameter of the circles you work to and the size of the cord, you may produce a flat circular unit of eight spokes as shown, but don't worry if you complete the unit in seven or even six spokes. Keep going; the spiral effect develops when you let the curved sennit hang free (123).

The above "twisties" can work well for necklaces or wall hangings, give interest to a fringe or a row of tassels, or you can make them out of gold or silver cord for ornaments.

Berry Knot. There are some combinations of square knots and clove hitches that are used enough to have been given a generally used name. The berry knot is one such example (124). With eight strands, numbered 1 through 8 from left to right, make a square knot to the right with #1 and #4 over #2 and #3. Make a square knot to the left with #8 and #5 over #7 and #6. Work the knots down so they lay diagonally as shown, and tie them tight. Using cords #5, #6, #7, and #8 in turn as the holding cords, clove hitch across each with #4, #3, #2, and #1 in turn. Tie a half knot to the left with #1 and #4 over #2 and #3. Tie a half knot to the right with #5 and #8 over #6 and #7. Pull both half knots tight and hold. With your finger, poke from the backside to raise the clove-hitched area and tightening the half knots more, complete them into square knots. This berry knot might be set off within a diamond of clove hitches, tied alternately, used singly in a fabric, or set along an 8-strand strap.

Weaving

There's one basic principle you should examine a bit further and that's weaving: plain, simple, over-one, under-one ordinary weaving (125). It's often worked into knotting projects, either within a specific area, perhaps out-

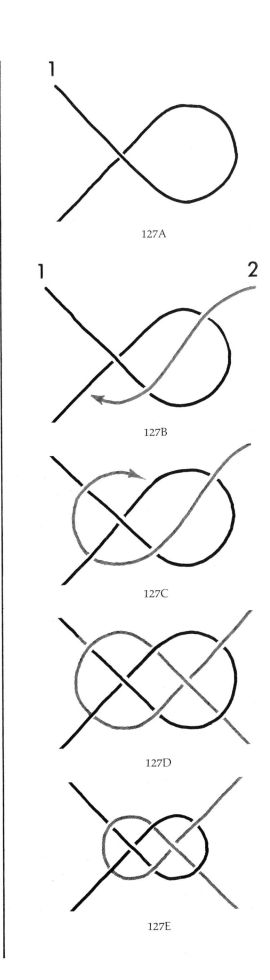

127A

127B

127C

127D

127E

128

129

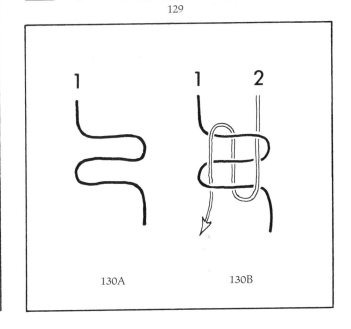

130A   130B

131. Traditional, nautical knotwork shows the use of an oriental temple knot and a cat-o'-nine-tails.

lined with clove hitching, or as a fabric for the bottom or sides of a project, or in the form of 3- or 4-strand flat braids to contrast the knotted sennits. Tying certain knots will be more easily understood, if the over-under sequence of weaving is kept in mind.

Everyone is familiar with the 3-strand and probably the 4-strand flat braids. Both are simple exercises in over-under intertwining and can be learned quickly if you follow the diagrams (126).

Carrick Bend. When you see that the carrick bend or Josephine knot is really one of the weavings, tying the knot becomes remarkably clean (127). First, lay out a loop (#1) as shown at A. Lay the second strand (#2) across it as shown in B. Run #2 under, then over #1 as in C. Take #2 under the top side of the first loop, over cord #2 itself, and under the far side of the #1 loop. When you've done it with a single cord, go on and use one, two, three, four, or more strands. The knot is tied exactly the same way. Pay attention, however, to keeping the strands flat and alongside each other when working the knot (128). It can be tied as a sennit, though when strain is applied it turns into a very strong but not particularly attractive knot once the flatness is disturbed.

Crown Knot. Another simple, woven knot is known by various names—crown knot, pillow knot, or success knot (129). Whatever you call it, squiggle down the left-hand cord (1) in a double loop. Weave the right-hand cord (2) under one, over two, up under all three, over two, under one, and out as shown by the double line (130). Work the knot tight. This is a useful center, can be tied doubled, and is the way old style Navy men tied their neckerchiefs into squarish-looking knots. The crown knot can be tied in an alternate arrangement, too, and makes a nice, light change—almost looking like netting when introduced into some projects. Getting it spaced properly may present difficulties; that's where pins help.

Oriental Knots

Weaving is the basis for many of the fancy oriental knots and quite a few of the nautical items once practical aboard ship such as the ones shown here (131).

Temple knots. Two oriental temple knots are diagrammed (132 and 133). Upside down either would make a necklace pendant. In stiff cord, with glued or sewn crossovers, they could be made to carry a dangling "jewel" or two. Tying both knots is simple if you follow the diagrams. Lay down the right-hand loop first, then the center, and then weave the end through, forming the left-hand loop so your layout agrees with A. Continue by weaving first one end and then the other as shown in B and C. Work the knot as tight as you want, always keeping it flat. Both knots shown work up well in multiple strands if you use reasonably stiff material. The photograph (134) shows braided nylon.

Some of the standard nautical mat designs can be use-

132A

133A

132B

133B

132C

133C

134

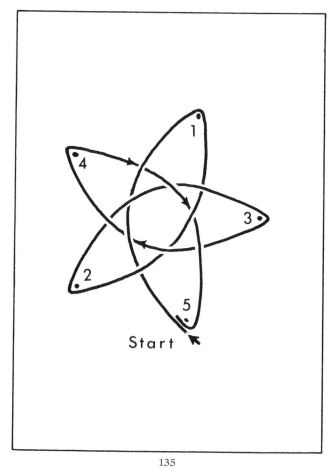

135

136

137

ful when worked in different sizes in other materials. Keep in mind the weaving syndrome at all times. The length of line needed to make a mat varies with the size of the line used and how many passes will be made with it, plus the fact that it has to be laid out loosely at first and then worked tight.

Turk's Head. The flat Turk's head is quick, simple, and good to start with (135). Put five pins in your knotting board, spaced equally around a circle. Start your cord alongside pin 5 and take it around pin 1, around pin 2, and around pin 3, laying the cord on top of each previous loop. On the way from pin 3 to pin 4, at the arrow, take the cord under the first segment laid. Then go on around pin 4. On the way to pin 5, lead the cord under both parts of the first loop which puts it over both parts of the third loop. When you round the loop at pin 5, you are alongside the starting point. Take a moment to follow the path with eye and finger. It should be under-over-under-over, right around. For a triple-passed Turk's head, take the cord two more times around the five pins, following exactly the same path but laying the cord down parallel to and inside the previous pass. When you've completed laying out the knot, remove the pins carefully and go around the knot to tighten it, one pass at a time, retracing the path you took laying it out. Tightening up the loops evenly will give you the size Turk's head you want (136).

Say you want to make a neckerchief slide and want to do it the easy way. When you remove the pins, gingerly pick up the knot and ease it over a dowel or paper tube the size you want the slide to be. It will look something like the photo, a real bird's nest. Ease the cords down so they run in waves around the tubular shape and then proceed one pass at a time to tighten them up (137). If you bring both ends to rest under what was the pin 1 to pin 2 section, they can be glued or sewn fast there quite unobtrusively and each visible segment will show the same number of cords.

Fancy Mat. The next mat shown could be a coaster, a pin, or an earring (138). To make it, lay out the cord in the configuration shown first at A, forming the right-hand shape first, then forming the left-hand one over it as in B. Bring the ends down through as indicated by the arrows in C. You'll come out with a single-strand version of the photo (139), loose and lumpy. Work it flat and lead one end around inside the first pass, the other end around always to the other side of the original line laid. You then have the same job of working out the slack all along the line, keeping the adjacent cords adjacent and not crossed over where they shouldn't be. Don't take it up too tightly however, or it will curl.

Turk's Head Variation. The time will come when you want to tie a Turk's head around something—a rail or handle—where you cannot slip the mat form on. There is a way (140). First, hold one end of the cord across the front of the rail diagonally as shown in A. Carry the other end over and behind the rail to the front again, crossing over

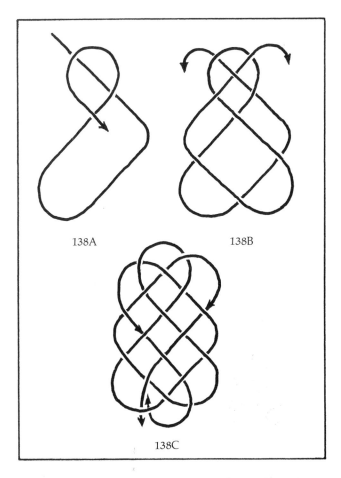

138A   138B

138C

139

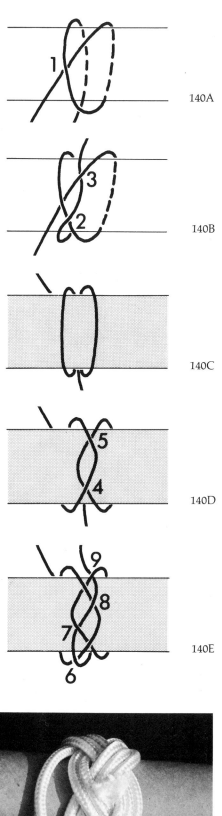

140A

140B

140C

140D

140E

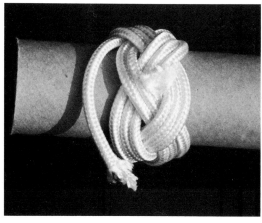

141

the first part at point 1. Go around the rail again and make a second crossing in front of you at point 2. Take the moving end under at point 3. All these crossings are shown in B. Peering over the rail, or rotating the knot formed towards you, the backside should look like the diagram at C. Slip the left-hand cord segment over the right-hand part to form the two crossings numbered 4 and 5 on the diagram at D. Now take the moving end over and under and over and under as shown in E at crossings numbers 6, 7, 8, and 9. Crossing number 10 will bring you alongside the starting end. Thread the moving end through twice more for a triple passed Turk's head. Working around a pass at a time as you did on the mats, tighten and even up the knot (141).

Monkey's Fist. The ball knot or monkey's fist is another embellishment often featured in macramé work (142-145). It requires fingers, patience, and the desire to work a Chinese puzzle through to the end. With the left hand, hold one end of the cord against the middle finger as in A and take three turns about the two fingers as shown. Then take the moving end around the strands as they pass the space between fingers, three strands on the palm side, three on the back, as shown in B and C. Finally, in C, take the moving end through the loops, alongside the forefinger. Dislodge the loops from both fingers and, holding them carefully, take the moving end through the bottom loops, around and through the top loops and alongside the first cord passed that way (143). Make that round twice more so you have three segments of cord at each positions. Tuck a bead in the hollow center of the cords, maintaining three turns at each crossing (144). The moving end should be tucked through as shown. Holding the starting end, work the whole thing tight over the bead, going along over the same trail one segment at a time (145). Make sure you don't allow any cords to go out of sequence. The ball can be used as a button or simply as decoration.

Nautical Embellishments

You may never need to cover a ship's rail, but some of the ornamental coverings make very attractive handles and certainly find a place as a heavier accent line in many hangings. One of the simplest is cockscombing. If you'll look back to the beginning of Chapter 2 you'll see immediately that you could substitute a rail for the inactive cord. Keep the hitches tight and even and the cord perfectly aligned for a simple but effective covering. Working with three cords instead of one (146) and hitching alternately right and left, you'll see a raised braided effect develop along the top edge of the rail. A good hint for starting is to hold the cord ends fast with tape. The proper nautical start and finish is, of course, not tape but whipping the end fast to the rail and covering it with a Turk's head (147). Depending on how and where you have done the hitching, wrapping (the same as for a tassel) is an effective finish, or if you've used the hitching

142A

142B

142C

143

144

145

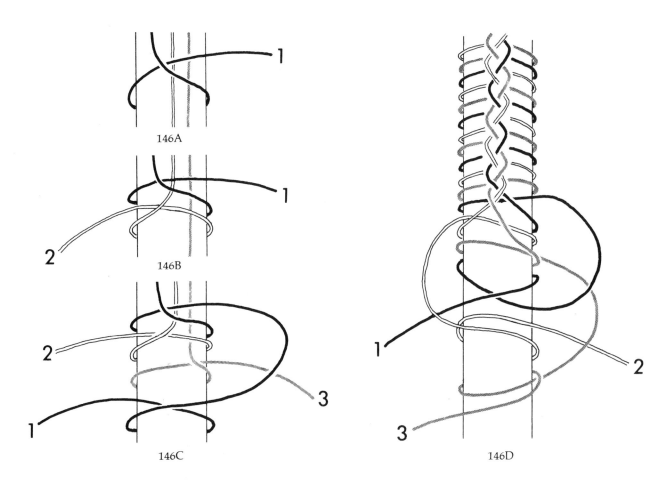

146A

146B

146C

146D

1 2 3 4

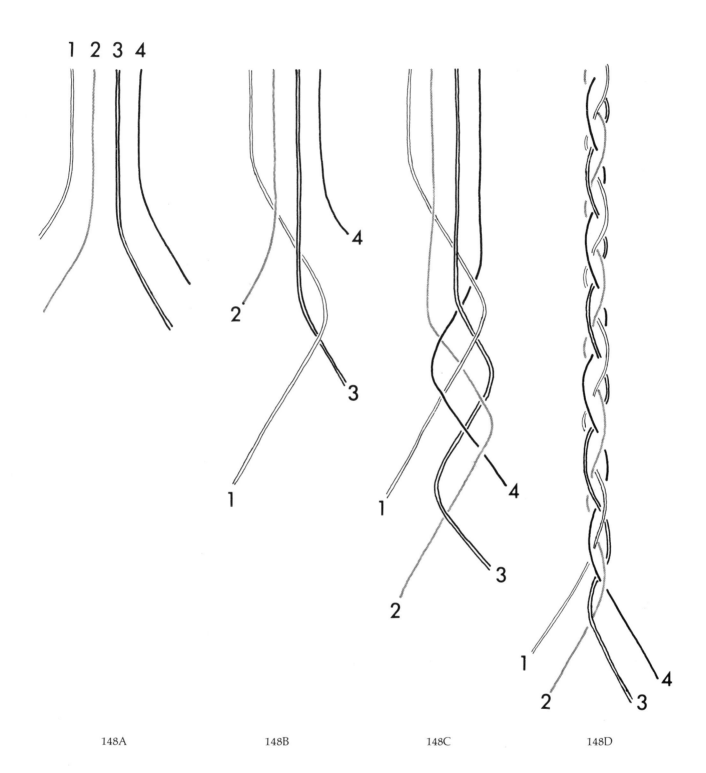

148A 148B 148C 148D

1 2 3 4 5 6 7 8

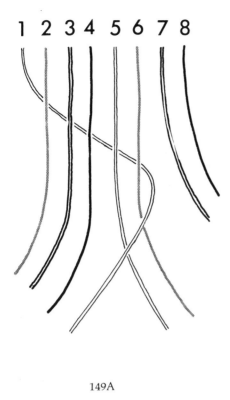

149A

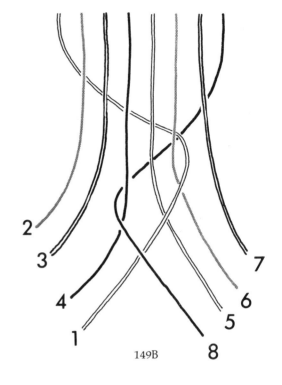

149B

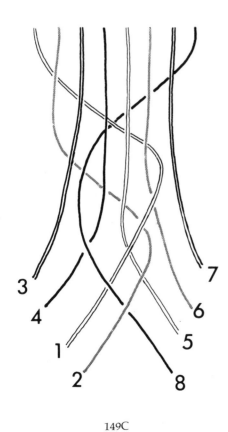

149C

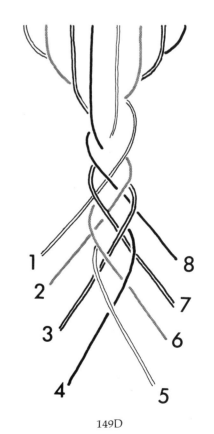

149D

around core cords for a handle, just bring each separate cord back into the body of the work. (See Chapter 4 for instructions on wrapping and whipping.)

There's no rule that says you have to work with three strands either; two, four, or five will also produce fine embellishments. You can also double the strands and work in pairs. As with the half-hitched sennits, you can vary the direction and number of strands hitched. For example, three strands hitched to the right can alternate with three to the left. Over ready-made rings, one of these designs often makes a neater handle than the bare material would and the ends serve as a means of attaching it to the rest of the macramé.

Sennit Braids. Other nautical-type items suitable for handles, lanyards, or accents include some of the sennit braids which are again a development of the over-under syndrome. The 4-strand sennit braid is quite effective when worked in two colors and is quite simple to do (148). The outside strand on the left is taken around behind the braid and between the two strands on the right to return to the left-hand side. The outside strand on the right goes behind the braid, between the two strands on the left, and back to the right, as shown.

Next try the 8-strand sennit. There is a key to this braid which must be remembered: when tying it, you must always maintain four cords on the right and four on the left. The method of tying is for the cord on the far left to pass under the cords to the right, come out in the middle of the group on the right, and loop back around to rejoin the group on the left. Then the cord on the far right does the same thing in the opposite direction. To understand it, pin and number your cords according to the diagram. Cord #1 passes under cords #2–#6 to the right, comes out between #6 and #7, and loops around cords #5 and #6 to the left (A). Then cord 8 passes under cords #7, #1, #6, #5, and #4 to the right, comes out between #3 and #4, and loops around cords #4 and #1 to the left. (B). Cords #2 and #7 follow the same procedure as shown in the diagram (C and D).

Crown Sennits. Related to the braided sennits are the crown sennit series (150). Wrap or tie the cords so you have a place to start from. Looking down the ends as the diagrams do, simply lay each strand (four, five, six or more) over the one next to it, threading the last one through the loop formed when the first is laid over. Continuing this in the same direction (working counterclockwise) results in a right-crown sennit. Clockwise it's a left-crown sennit, or alternating the direction is an alternate-crown sennit, if the names matter. The looks change. These crown sennits are hollow and can (and if you use over six strands it should) be tied over a core of some sort which you may or may not remove.

The braids, fancy knots, mats, and sennits discussed here are just the tip of the iceberg—there are infinitely more. If, for you, doing your own thing in macramé means investigating further, then check out the bibliography.

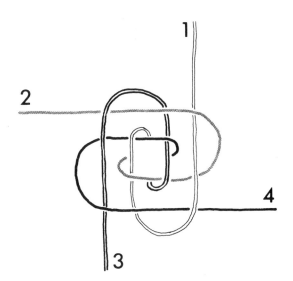

150A

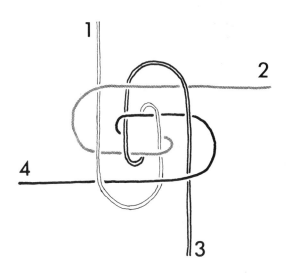

150B

6. Adding and Subtracting

The practical problem of the too-short cord often occurs in macramé. This can happen when your initial figures are wrong or when the cord is cut too short. If you're working freely, this problem also crops up when the design develops an unexpected need. Whatever the cause, the problem of the too-short cord means that one or more cords just aren't long enough to complete the work.

Adding in Square-Knotted Work

Whenever possible, anticipate the need for adding a cord far enough in advance to find an unobtrusive point to hide the operation. In square knotting with a 3- or 4-knot sennit, it's simple to have three cords in the core at a time (151). Overlap the new end with the old one so the overlap is enveloped in the knotting cords and hidden from view.

If the cord is small, or of a quality where two cords can be worked up nearly as small as one, adding in a working cord is also possible (152). Let the two ends overlap and knot both as one for a few knots.

In alternating square knot patterns, one solution is to insert the new cord in the core, tie the next knot with the two cords worked as one, and let both ends go free behind the work to be tied off and cut later (153).

Where the cord size is too large to do any of these things, pin the new end out away from the work. Then tie the new cord into the next knot, dropping the end of the too-short cord (154). The pin can be removed a few rows further on. When the project is complete, work back and tie off the ends on the reverse side.

Sometimes, in very large cordage, the cord can be spliced if you have the patience and know-how of an old-line seaman. Or you can fake the splice in some cords by gluing and twisting the unlaid ends together.

Adding into Clove Hitches

In tightly clove-hitched areas, adding a cord can be done a number of ways. If the cord is fuzzy or soft and it's difficult to count the number of clove hitches in a row, simply pin the new end securely and clove hitch it on the holding cord next to the last hitch made with the too-short cord. Later, tie off or glue the ends and work them in on the reverse side.

If you can count the hitches, it's a bit less obvious if you make only one hitch (the first half of a clove hitch)

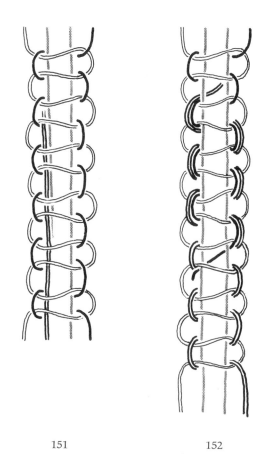

151   152

with the too-short cord and one hitch with the new end around the holding cord, making one clove hitch (155). You can leave the ends for later. In both methods, later rows lock the cords in place quite securely.

Where the addition can be made in the holding cord, simple overlapping suffices; just try to do it in the middle rather than the last few clove hitches of a given row (156). If there's no strain on the cord, the ends can be buried in the knots. Otherwise find the ends and work them back in on the reverse side.

Adding Cords (Planned)

It's quite possible to add cords to increase the size of a piece, change the color, alter the design, make the piece three dimensional, or to branch off in some other manner.

Square-Knotted Work In square-knotted work, it's best to add two, four, or a multiple of four cords in each row of knotting. If you refer back to the starting methods, it's easy to see that if you want to add two cords in an alternating square-knotted piece, the method used to start from a point is applicable. It can be repeated in later rows

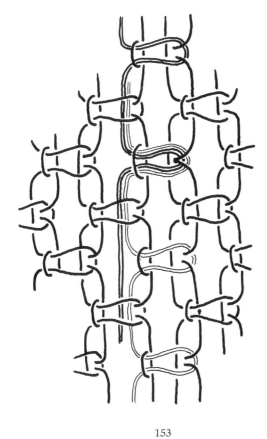

153

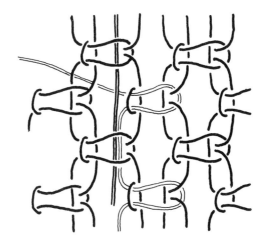

154

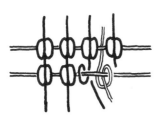

155A

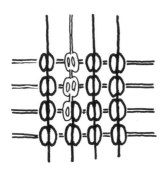

155B

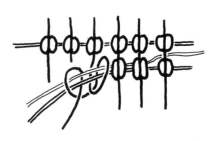

156

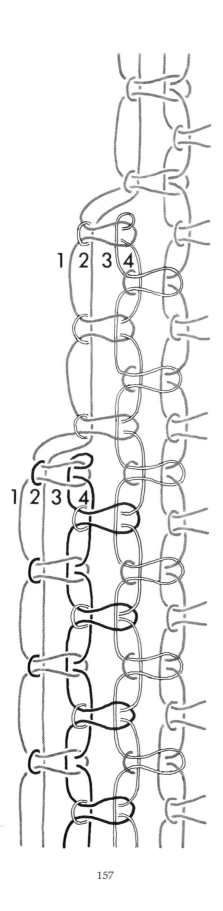

157

as many times as required. If the loop sticking out is objectionable, adding the doubled length in the 3–4 position is equally simple (157).

When the starting cord is carried vertically past the square-knotted area, the alternate rows can very easily lark's head over it (158). You can add the new doubled cord as one of the lark's heads, then tie into the alternating pattern as before. This works particularly well where a second cord is run parallel to the starting cord to control spacing.

If more fullness is desired in the center of the square-knotted area, adding four working cords closer together may be more successful. Pin on two additional loops and tie into the work, actually forming an extra row (159). The next regular row will then pick up the additional knots.

Lark's heads can also be used to add on in the center of a piece (160). Knot a pair of doubled cords over adjacent pairs of core cords, bringing the additional cords into the next alternating row. Or lark's head both doubled cords over the square knot center in one row, tying the additional square knot in line with the next row down.

The same pattern of attachment can be done by simply looping the added cords through as shown (161), but then it's necessary to guard against loosing the center of the cords as you knot.

To add what amounts to a gusset, consider one area as being turned and add to the side of it as many new cords as are required. The simplest method is to attach them with lark's heads (162).

Clove-Hitched Work. Adding on in tightly clove-hitched work is even simpler. Pin the end of a new cord fast and clove hitch it in around the holding cord (163). Work the extra end in later.

The holding cord may be extended and new doubled cords added with a picot. Where holding cords cross, new cords can be added with lark's head clove hitched into the next row.

Laying in a new holding cord, which becomes new working cords on either or both ends is an easy and most satisfactory way to add in solid color work (164).

It's obvious that many such planned additions must be considered as part of the larger design, particularly where colors are used. It should be remembered that the color of the holding cord, perhaps hidden for rows, can be made to surface simply by making the holding cord the knotting cord.

Circular Work. Adding in circular pieces is possible by adapting most of the methods just described. You can also add another circle and start again from that, clove hitching the existing cords and using lark's heads to attach new ones at regular intervals (165). It's useful for projects such as the hat shown (166).

With solid clove hitching in a circle, a spiral holding cord can be used. Cords added with a single hitch in one round are picked up with the clove hitching in the next.

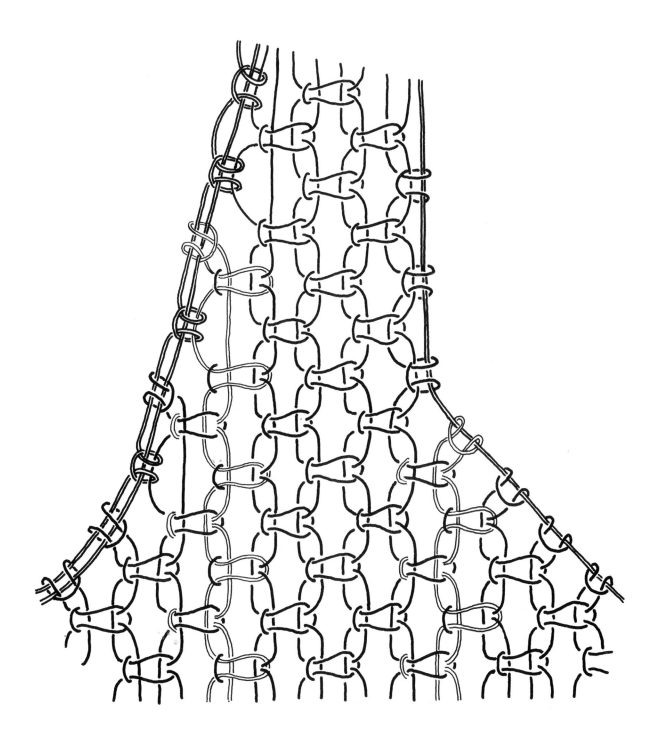

158

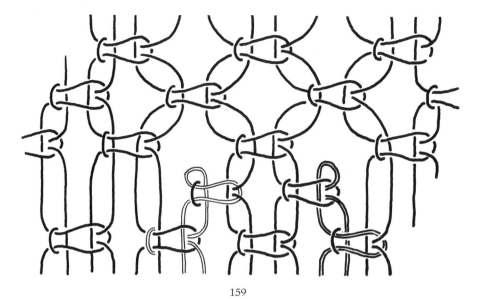

159

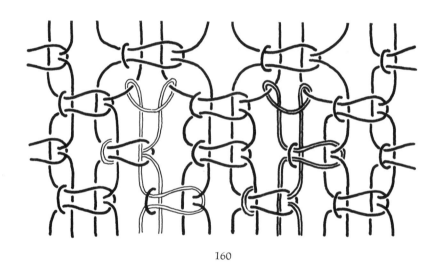

160

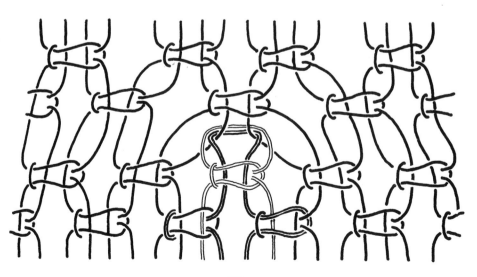

161

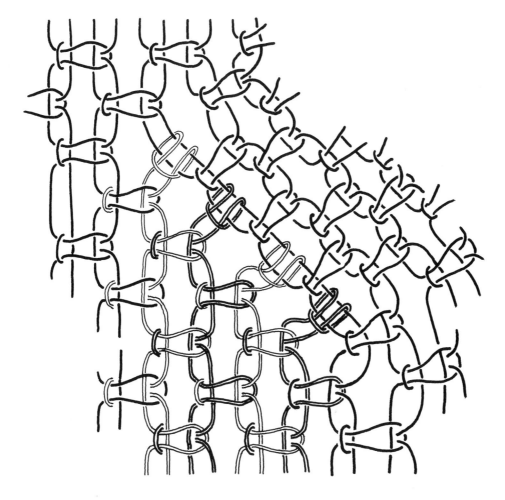

162

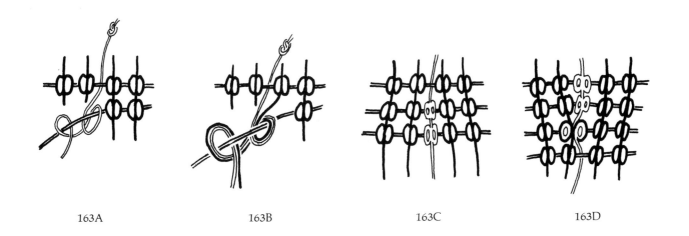

163A   163B   163C   163D

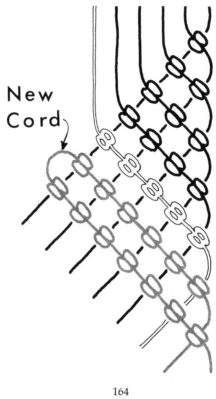

New
Cord

164

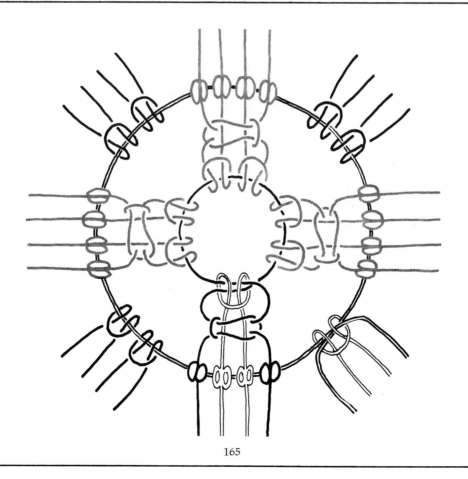

165

166. A hat that was started from a ring at the crown and then worked outwards.

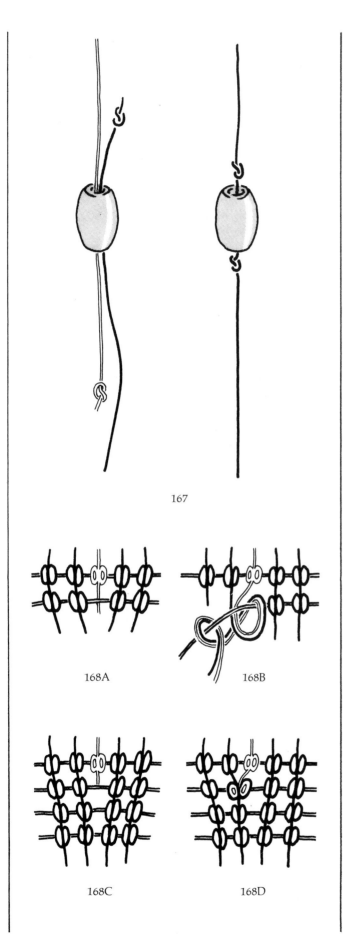

167

168A

168B

168C

168D

Adding with Beads. Any construction method that works can become a design element by accenting it with color, scale, or repetition. The working in of construction necessities is one of the most challenging aspects of macramé. You can make a feature of even the too-short cord problem. Here are a couple of "flaunt it" methods; they work for adding cords and solving the too-short problem.

Design a pattern of beads into your piece, based on the location of the too-short cord. Tie an overhand knot at the end of the new cord and thread the cord through a bead. Then thread the end of the too-short cord through the bead from the other side. Tie an overhand knot in the too-short cord tight below the bead, glue, and clip the end off evenly (167). On the other cords in the design, tie an overhand knot, thread on a bead in line with the patching bead, and tie another overhand knot beneath it. Only close inpsection will show which bead hides the added replacement cord. The same idea can be done with wrapping the overlapped cords, clipping the ends off short above and below the finished wrapping.

To add new cords, you simply have one cord going into the bead at the top and two coming out the bottom. The same thing happens with the wrapping method: an overhand knot at the end of the new cord above the wrap holds it.

Subtracting

There are two possible attitudes to take when there are more cords than desired at a given point: either allow them to disappear, or make a focal point or feature out of their ending. When a gradual narrowing effect is desired, particularly in wearing apparel, it's the less obvious way that's usually used. Bring the two cords together and knot them as if they were one cord for a knot or two, then drop the unwanted cord (168). Naturally this should be done in an organized way to get a balanced result. Subtracting a number of cords in a relatively close area is a maneuver that borders on three dimensional work because it's very hard to control the flatness.

One possible feature element is deliberate tasseling introduced into the body of a piece (169). Four cords can sennit and then form a tassel, or you could use only the core cords, or only the knotting cords. Whatever is left under the tassel, however, must be a proper multiple to continue the alternating square knot work.

An alternate way might be to bead the ends or barrel knot them for an interesting textural look. If your decreasing can be done in a row, you could form two layers and produce a knotted fringe on the surface while the main body of the work continues on beneath it.

All the methods for adding and subtracting can lead into three-dimensional work. The cords brought forward to drop can just as easily become a textural feature or fringe. In the same way a sennit can be brought forward as a design element (170) and then be worked back into the fabric again.

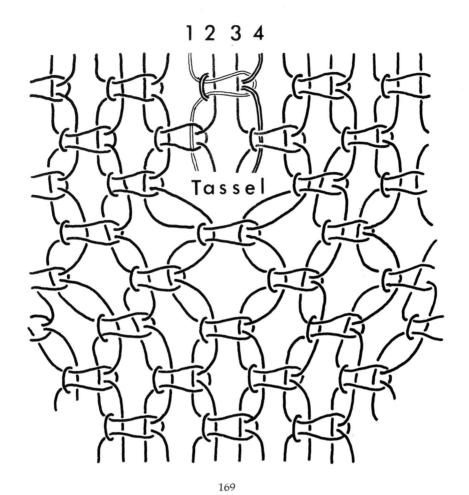

1 2 3 4

Tassel

169

170

7. Making Shapes

Going three dimensional is the next natural step. This chapter, then, has to be a short review of plane and solid geometry, paying special attention to the top, bottom, and side joints of a piece. It will also include how basic shapes can be used to make macramé projects, both practical and just pretty. Once you begin to think in terms of shape, making a particular thing or covering a specific object will become subject to endless possibilities. That's why sculptural macramé is such an inventive area for investigation. You can discover myriad shapes by turning a simple strap and working it back into the fabric. Familiarity with how knotted shapes are developed will suggest solutions to practical pieces and planned shapes will often lead you on to many interesting sculptural forms. Even before you consider the simplest shape, the rectangle, there is one question that always has to be answered: "Where do you want the fringe?" If you think the answer to the question is always "at the bottom," take a look at the four bottles shown (171–174). Example A was started at the top and fringed at the bottom with the ends pasted flat and covered by felt (171). Example B was started at the bottom and allowed to braid off and fringe around the top (172). Example C was started at both the top and bottom and then fringed where the two parts met in the middle (173). Example D was started with the work center at one side of the bottle and fringed along the opposite side (174). So there's more than one way to skin a cat or cover a bottle. We might also have covered a fifth bottle, starting in the middle and working both up and down.

The Rectangle

Take a good look at bottle D. This can be seen as a rectangular shape molded to conform to the bottle covered. You made rectangles in Chapter 1 (straps are long skinny rectangles) and you've already manipulated a strap into a three-dimensional shape in the slip-over necklace idea. You'll find that there are any number of things you can do with a rectangle without manipulating it (175). It can be started at the center and fringed at opposite sides, or started at one side or end and fringed at the other. It could also be started at both sides, knotted together down the center, and if you explore the possibilities of the 45° angle, it becomes apparent that it could be started in the center and fringed on all four sides.

A rectangle can be a stole if properly proportioned and made of suitable materials. Put a hole in the middle and

171

172

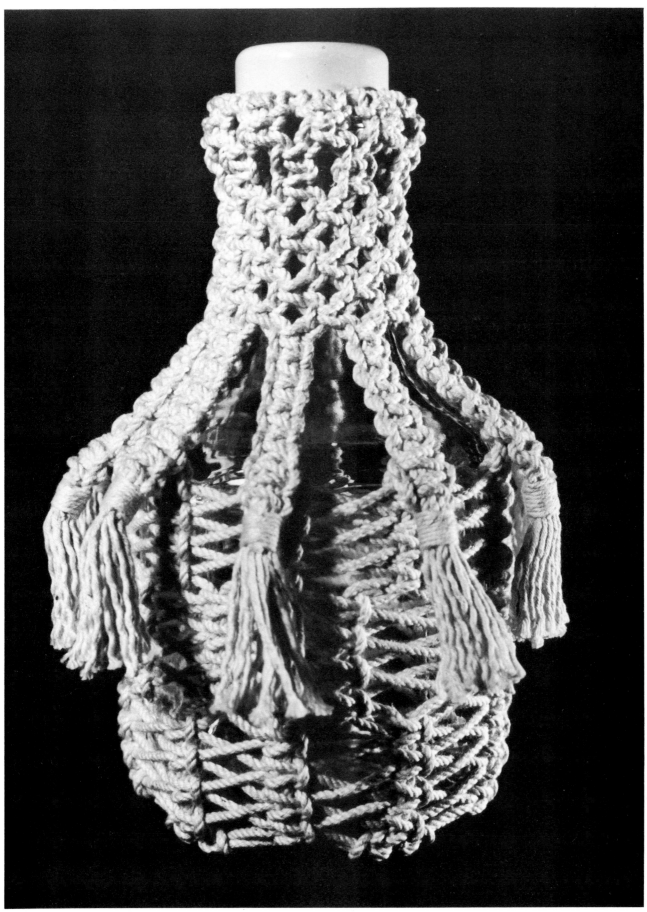

173

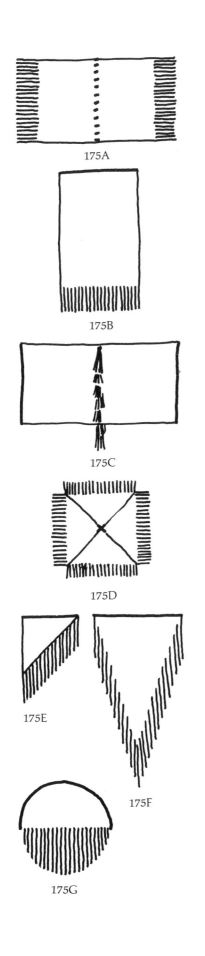

175A

175B

175C

175D

175E

175F

175G

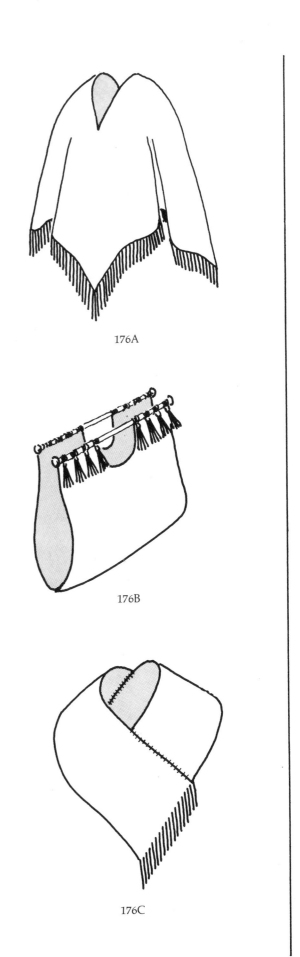

176A

176B

176C

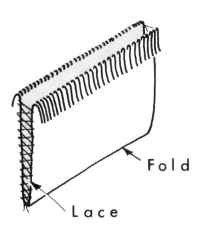

Fold

Lace

177A

Fold

Lace

Fold

177B

178

it's a poncho. Take two rectangles, seam the ends and sides together and you have a different style of poncho. Mounted, it's a pillow front, a chair, or stool seat. It's certainly a mat or table runner. With a handle at both ends it's a log tote or a book or package carrier, especially if the knotting pattern is an expanding one (176).

Folding a rectangle and lacing it up the side is the next step (177). Folded once, you have a two-seam envelope, open at the top and fringed all around if you started the rectangle in the middle. Start the rectangle at one end, work flat to the fringe, fold as shown, and you have a flap to close over the top of a bag seamed up the sides. The bag (178) shows the strap knotted in place after the sides were seamed.

Within the flat rectangle you have many possible shapes: triangle, sawtooth, pennant, or banner. Macramé is flexible enough to work into curved shapes, too. You can make a vest front by shaping the right-hand and left-hand pieces to a dress pattern. Attach them to a leather or fabric back section and you've started making wearing apparel.

The Cylinder

Macramé is endlessly tubular too. Tubular suggests cylindrical and right away you think of lampshades, wastebaskets, bottles, round hassocks, and certainly sculptural hangings. All are projects that cover, or start from, a circular shape. You could start at the top, the bottom, or go both ways from the middle for a round bolster cover tasseled and fringed at both ends (179).

A waistline is circular too, so skirts and aprons are the next possibility. You'll have to beware of the weight and expansion peculiarities of macramé though. Spaced alternating square knots cling-fit, seeking their own equilibrium. They tend to fall straight down from the weight of the cord, unless the hips or some form of hoop is used to keep the horizontal spacing constant. You may have discovered this already and it's one of the reasons for investigating the intertwined fabrics. A single sennit hangs down straight and two sennits tied together tend to hang together.

Consider the folded envelope made by lacing up a folded flat rectangle. A rectangle worked both ways from the center can be folded right away into a cylindrical form which will give you the same envelope with fringe around the open edges. In alternating square knots this is quite easily done with very little adjustment needed at the turned corners.

You can make the tube, folded flat, with the fringe at the bottom too (180A). Tie the starting line completely around your knotting board. Work the cylinder down from that, shifting the piece as you work or turning the board over. Tie the fringe together, one or two strands from the back with one or two from the front and you have the shape closed at the bottom.

Consider going both ways from the starting line across the back for a flapped bag (180B).

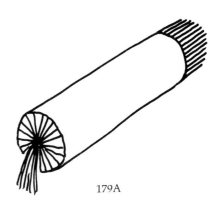

179A

179B

179C

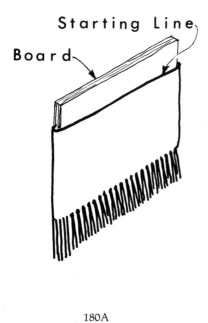

180A

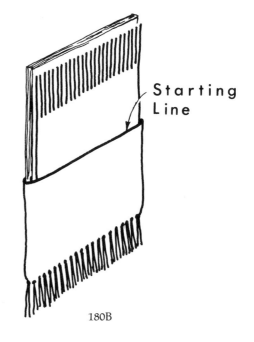

180B

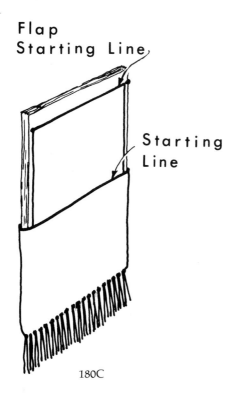

180C

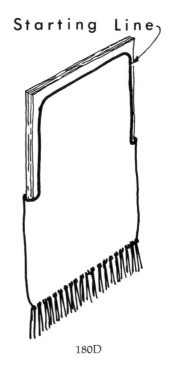

180D

This well may be the place to note the meandering or dual purpose starting line. We might use the envelope-with-flap-style purse to clarify this. If you want a flap without fringe, then you need a holding line at the bottom of the flap (either that or tuck all those ends under). But you also want a holding line at the opening of the bag, having found what a chore it is to work all the fringe ends neatly under at that point. There are two ways you can do this. If you consider the bag portion as starting from a cylindrical line and the flap starting from its own starting line, the cords of the flap can be clove hitched about the bag line as they encounter it (180C). The other way is to make the starting line for the flap turn and turn again to become the holding line for the open edge of the bag (180D). This is the general approach used in the tailored bag shown (181–183).

Most bag plans can easily combine a built-in strap for handles or a shoulder strap, depending on the style of bag desired (184). Make a strap or sennit first, then joining both ends to the starting line with clove hitches. This built-in handle is somewhat stronger than the separately made, tied-on variety. There are, of course, many types of fittings for bags that substitute for starting lines. These will be discussed in Chapter 9.

If the fringe is at the top of the bag and you want a handle or two there are several ways to do it. Elongated fringe can be braided or knotted and tied back into the bag only at one end. Or two areas of elongated fringe can be combined, either by knotting them together or by working one around the other, and then tied back into the bag at the opposite end. The photo (185) may help clarify this.

The Circle

Back to the cylinder as a tubular shape. If you put a bottom in a cylindrical tube of macramé you can space the verticals to be equidistant around a circle. This will overcome the sag factor in spaced knotting to a degree. Also, if you clove hitch the cords over a ring every few rows of knotting, you can use this sag factor to advantage in sculptural designs.

Put a bottom of a solid material (cut off a bleach bottle to make the bottom of a beach bag, for instance), plan a drawstring top, and you've made a bag a different way. Or you could fill the bottom in with a macramé circle.

As a flat shape a circle can grow in diameter by adding cords, as seen in Chapter 4. It can also be done as an ending system, subtracting cords to decrease the diameter of the circle, and then it becomes a conical shape. As the bottom of a drawstring bag, the radially arranged cords turn up and the shape becomes tubular. As the top of a hat, the shaped circle can develop in either direction, inward to an elastic for a tam o'shanter or outward to a stiff or droopy brim. Or start with the outside diameter and work into a center pom-pom. Or a hat can go both ways from the middle—up into a cone shape and out into a circle.

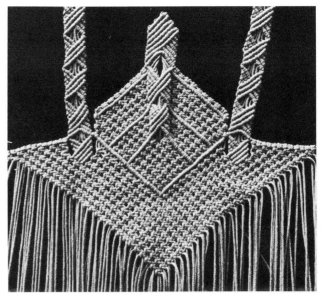

181

182

183

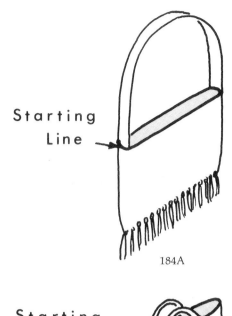

Starting
Line

184A

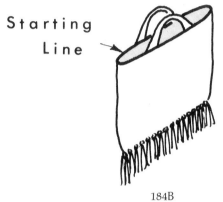

Starting
Line

184B

185

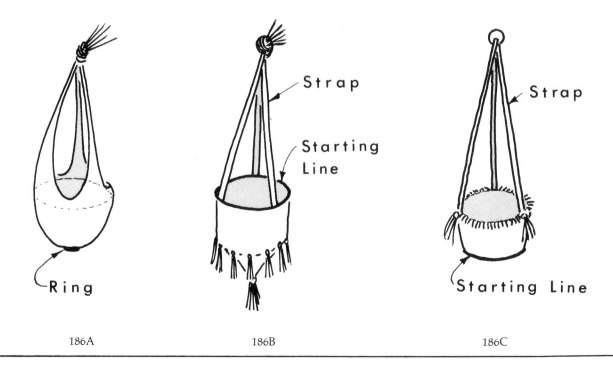

Ring

186A

Strap

Starting
Line

186B

Strap

Starting Line

186C

The Triangle

A planter hanger is easily made by knotting a circular shape with the strands running up to a central suspending clump at the top, shaped as required to fit the container (186A). You'll get a smaller clump at the top if you tassel off a few strands before you get there. You can work the other way also, by considering a hanger as a series of straps joined to a tubular shape at the bottom (186B). You can work the hanger in two sections as well—straps down and cone up—to get the fringe in the middle about even with the rim of the container (186C). There's a lot to be said for this approach: the decoration is where you want it, the suspension portion light and lineal, and no possibly wet tassel need be under the drain hole at the bottom.

There are two practical considerations to make in suspending a weight like this. First, study the suspension system. The core cords will stretch only as much as the material they're made of and the knotting cords will take up slack when weight is applied. Popcorn sennits or carrick bends don't make the best suspension sennits because they tend to stretch and deform under tension. The second consideration is a case of balance. Two points will tip, while four will teeter if they're not all exactly equal, but a triangle is self centering. Using three sennits to suspend something will divide up the weight to be carried so all lines are under equal tension. Use four, and one will almost always go slack. Again, this a consideration for design ideas. For example you could use three straight lines and three in-between that are allowed to go slack. Use your imagination along with your common sense.

Box Shapes

Macramé is flexible. You can change the cross section of the tubular macramé from round to square or rectangular. In fact, if you build in a wide strap on your shoulder bag, the tubular shape tends to become rectangular of its own accord. So you come to the next obvious shape—the box. Start with a rectangular bottom, fold up the four sides, and then go tubular with the fringe around the top (187). Start with a rectangular tube, join on the 45° diagonals at the bottom, and your bag can have a shape like an upside down roof or an upside down pyramid if your cross section is square (188). You can leave the fringe outside as you decrease, or bring the dropped ends inside and keep them invisible. If you find the right number of cords to subtract in each row for the pattern you're tying you can get a flat bottom.

Variations

All other shapes in macramé will be subtle variations of round and rectangular tubes, cones, and pyramids. Straps joined to three-dimensional tubular shapes enable you to construct just about anything you'd want to make in macramé (189). What is a bra top but two cones and a few straps? Pants might be a cylinder slit front and a back, fringed to join at the crotch. Then you would add more cords to make the two cylinders necessary for the legs. For a bikini, a shaped rectangle laced together at the sides might be a better approach.

You'll find other wearing apparel and accessories reducible to one of these general shapes.

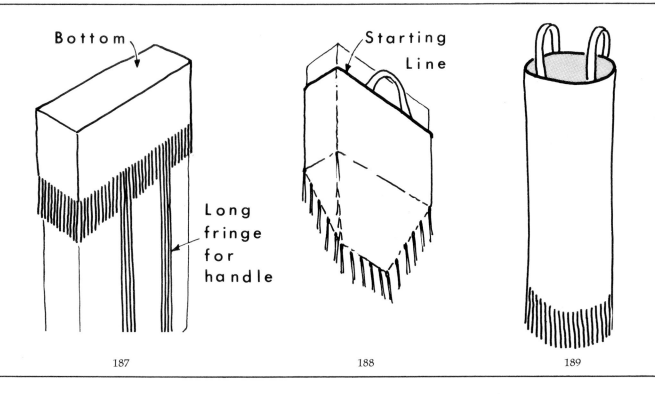

Bottom

Long fringe for handle

187

Starting Line

188

189

8. Materials and Estimating

There are many materials you can tie knots with (190). First there are the natural ones such as cotton, jute, sisal, and linen. Natural fibers are obtained from plants: cotton from the seed pods of the cotton plant; jute from the inner bark of an Asiatic herb; sisal from the leaves of a West Indian agave; and linen from flax. They're then processed into strands in which the fibers lay parallel to each other. These twisted strands are themselves twisted or twined around each other to produce thread, string, twine, cord, and, if it's over 1" in diameter, rope. These can be of 2, 3, 4, 5 or more plies. Strands of various materials may also be braided into tubular cording, with or without a core (191). Synthetic fibers are usually continuous filaments which can be used as is, twisted into a cord, or braided. Yarn is a spun fiber that's looser than a twisted one and made of a number of materials: animal, plant, or synthetic. Some other materials to consider are leather thongs, plastic lacing, raffia (strips of the fibrous leaves of a cultivated palm), and even very flexible wire.

Cord Qualities

Generally in macramé you want a cord that keeps its identity so the knots can become the design feature. For example, if you knit an angora sweater you lose the looks of the yarn itself in the finished product. You could do the same in macramé, but it's generally accepted that the knotting pattern is the important feature—not an area of fuzzy texture. That's not to say you shouldn't use angora yarn if it's the look you want.

Sometimes you'll want a cord that's comfortable against the skin for apparel, necklaces, or purses. Other times strength and tension are more important. The weathering qualities of cords that are to be exposed outdoors can also be a factor. Stretch or stiffness is something else that has to be considered in some projects. For example, the butterfly variation of the square knot doesn't look like much in a limp cord; it takes a certain stiffness of cord for it to really show up.

Weight is another consideration in selecting cord. Some cords are just too heavy for apparel or for large bags. A string tote should be knotted in a light cord and open design so you only carry a bit more than the weight you put in it. A seat mat, however, can take a heavy cord and is more comfortable if worked in a tightly knotted pattern. For learning you'll want a cord that won't fray when you pick out mistied knots. For fast work you'll want a cord that gives little or no trouble with slippage when the knots are formed.

Color and Finish

For any project you need to consider color, and dyeing cords to suit you is a process in itself. Most of the fabric dyes work on most cords. The big problem is deciding when to dye. If you dye cord and then cut and ravel, you might get an unattractive end that shows the undyed inner fibers. If you do want to dye, prepare your dye solution according to the manufacturer's directions or to your book of instructions for natural dyes.

Another method of dyeing produces slightly different results. Finish the article first, then dye it as you would any other completed piece. The problem here is that the cord color may show after the dyed knot has tightened up. Also, with hot dye baths there may be a degree of shrinkage. This isn't critical unless it affects a made-to-size item. An additional warning—some glues soften with boiling water and it's advisable to take needle and thread to secure the critical knots. As more and more manufacturers realize there is a market for more colorful cords, your need to dye will be decreased.

When looking at colored cords to buy, do examine them thoroughly. There are some manufacturers who haven't licked the penetration problem and their cord is still a natural color in the inner fibers. Some of the braided cords have a core of white or some other color than the braided exterior.

One other consideration is the finish. Some cords are waxed, oiled, starched, or otherwise "fixed"; some marine supplies are tarred; some farm and garden supplies may be impregnated with mildew and rot preventatives. Such treatments may or may not be desirable, so be aware of what you're buying.

Cost

Another important consideration is cost. Generally speaking, larger amounts of cord give a lower cost per foot. Cords bought in hardware or discount stores are apt to be less expensive than the same thing bought in specialty shops. It's a good idea to check out mail order prices and compare them with what's available in your own area. When you find a big ball of 5-ply jute at the stationery store is less expensive than two small balls of hardware store garden twine, it's rewarding. Look around. Hardware, stationery, garden supply, sporting goods, variety, and discount stores, art–needlework departments, yard goods, trimmings, and housewares sections of dime stores and supermarkets are all good hunt-

190

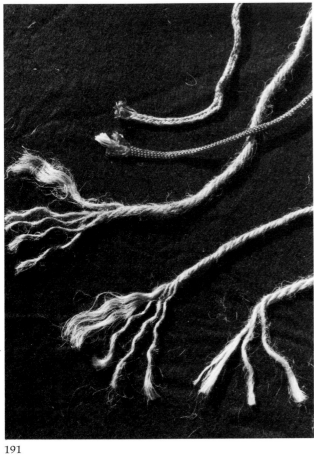

191

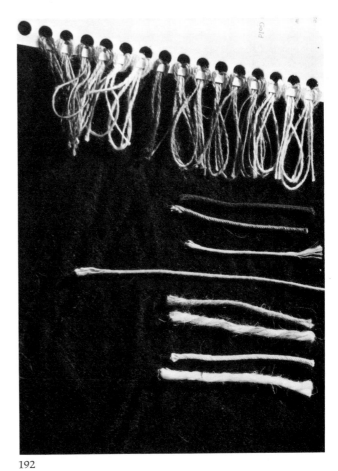

192

ing grounds, as well as yarn centers, weaving supply houses, and shops specializing in crafts and macramé supplies.

Cord Properties

It's often helpful to know what the properties are of the different yarns you'll be using.

Flax. The fibers of the flax plant are comparatively long, which makes linen cords relatively strong (192). The natural shade is a grayish tan, but some weaving yarns are available in very attractive and unusual tones. It's a bit small in size for macramé, but is sometimes useful for jewelry or other fine work. There is also a linen twine, #36, available in a good range of colors, but it's terribly expensive. However, there's a sheen to linen that doesn't exist in any other cord, so there will be times when you'll want to use it.

Jute. Jute is fuzzier than linen, much less expensive, and comes in various grades (193). Hardware store jute is usually 3-ply and inexpensive enough for large projects. The heavier 5-ply jute from stationery stores knots up fast with very little fuzziness. Colored 2-ply jute is available nationally and is quite even in quality, but contributes a lot of fuzz as you work with it. Jute is also not the longest lasting cord to use, but its natural tone—a sandy colored light brown—goes well with natural objects such as branches, rusty things, shells, and stones.

Cotton. Cotton fibers are shorter in their natural state than either jute or linen and require more of a twist to get them to stay together to form a strand (194). Single-ply cotton string is a loose, puffy cord used for upholsterers welting and butcher's string. It can be interesting and comfortable for wearing apparel where softness is desired. The size range is extensive and you'll find this type of cording in good quality at fabric centers rather than hardware stores. It's also available from weaving supply houses in a slightly harder twist.

Seine Twine and Mason's Line. More often the cotton cord you'll use is the mason's line or seine twine variety. Each ply has a harder twist and each cord has a harder lay which makes the cord comparatively stiff. Good quality cotton seine cord is available in #18, #36, and #72 sizes at hardware and department stores and building supply centers. It's also available in colors from some macramé suppliers. Seine cord can be washed in fabric softener to get rid of some of its stiffness. Relatively inexpensive, it's useful for bags, belts, footwear, and certainly for hangings. It's a good choice for involved macramé designs where you want the knotting to be really important and in #36 it's great for learning knots.

Braided Cotton. Glazed braided cotton is marketed for Venetian blind cord and traverse line; when the stiffener is left out of the cord, the same manufacturer has a natural product for macramé. It comes in a small size and color range, is flexible, and the braid with a core holds its shape. Cotton tubular braid without a core is quite limp and very good for wearing apparel. More expensive than twine, the color range is steadily improving and it has none of the right- or left-handedness in the finished look of the knots that you get with seine twine.

Waxed Cotton Cords. Waxed colored cotton cords are of a small diameter and particularly good for men's wear.

Sisal. Another natural fiber, sisal, is made in 2 or more ply (195). It's quite stiff and scratchy and has a mind of its own as far as falling straight goes. The scratchiness of working with it makes it uncomfortable for those with tender skin, but its stiffness makes it good for sculptural pieces. The natural color is a light straw, though there are some imports in red and green.

Synthetic Cords

There are many types of synthetic cord available to the macramé enthusiast. Some are manufactured especially for macramé and others have been borrowed from various industries, but each has a unique quality.

Rayon. Long available to the trimming industry, this 2- and 3-ply twine comes in a wide range of colors and can be found at some yarn outlets and specialty shops. It can also be obtained by mail order (196). It works up fairly well and has a richer sheen than cotton. There are braided rayon cords, too, but they're mostly drapable (limp) rather than stiff.

Rattail. Another rayon, rattail, is in a class by itself. Comparatively expensive, the sheen and color range make it delightful for jewelry, fancy sashes, and small bags. It's slippery to knot, but the larger size can be tacked fast with a needle and thread. The ends may cause problems, as well, but a barrel knot dipped in glue and water is an easy solution. Some brands aren't guaranteed colorfast, which might be a problem.

Rayon Braid. There are some fancy forms of rayon braid used for trimmings that are available by the yard in variety stores and notions departments. Gold cord and fancy flat braids are examples, and some may be very useful for certain decorative projects.

Nylon and Mason's Cord. Another synthetic, nylon, is available as twine or braided cord (197). Nylon itself is elastic and some of the twine is quite stretchy. You may experience some slipperiness, but applying heat will seal the knots. Put aluminum foil over the back of your work and press with a hot iron. The foil keeps the nylon off your iron and a little experimenting will show you how long to press to get the desired result. Colored nylon braid is available in a good range of shades in specialty shops. White and a brassy gold is also available in the form of mason's cord at your hardware store. The ma-

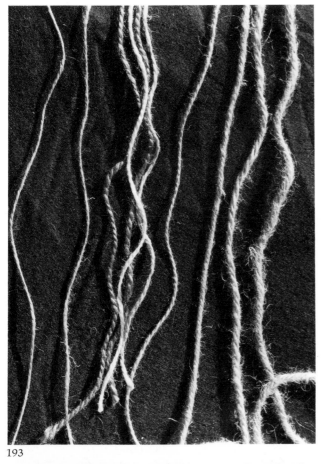

193

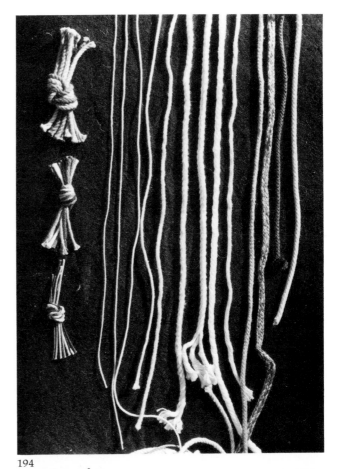

194

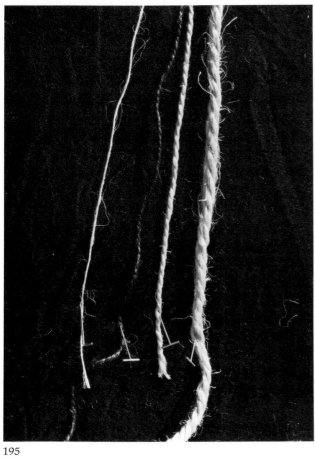

195

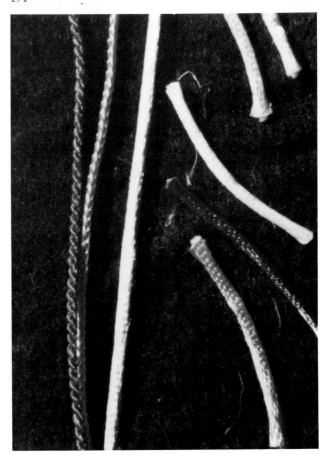

196

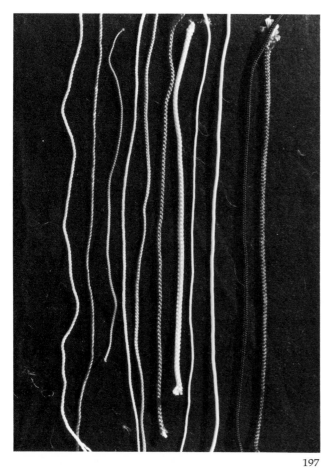

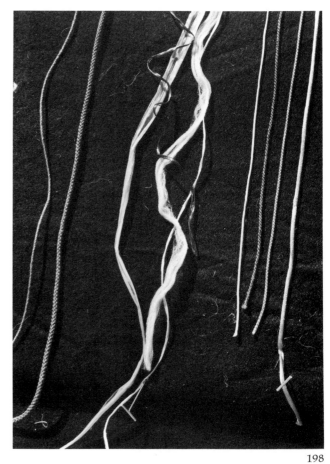

197

198

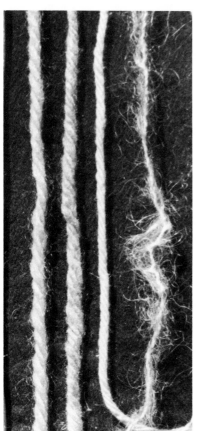

199

200

son's cord has a rougher weave and seems to knot more securely. Large-size nylon flat braid with a core makes great looking bags, but weigh it before you buy it; it's heavy.

Polypropelyne and Polyolefin. These synthetics start out as continuous filaments (198). Polypropelyne comes in a braided form in excellent colors (and colorfast too) but is very expensive per yard. One form works up quickly due to its size (almost ⅛" in diameter) and the braided surface texture holds knots well. Cut, fringed, and steamed it makes great puffy ends. There's a polyolefin that comes in 325-yard packages in an excellent range of colors. It's small in size, 4-ply, and quite stiff to handle, but is sometimes useful. Pull the knots hard and tight to have them hold well.

Twisted polypropylene clothesline (2-ply) is next to impossible to work with. The knots won't hold and the stuff is quite stiff, but there may be other manufacturers that offer this type of cord with different qualities. The one good thing about poly is its color retention outdoors.

The process of polymerization also offers some unusual varieties of yarn made primarily for knitting and crocheting. A ribbon form, similar to natural raffia in looks, is strong and available in a variety of colors. When you knot it, the broad flat "yarn" condenses and the knots become quite small, but it's not expensive and certainly worth experimenting with. Another form is floaty and light, but, again, the knots condense as you work it. In a pile, loose, it looks like cotton candy. The color range of both forms is a joy and you'll find them in art needlework centers and yarn stores.

Yarns

Yarn is another thing entirely. Most yarns for knitting and crocheting are too stretchy to make good macramé cords and compact too much while knotting to work out well. However, you may find you like some fluffy yarn or even roving (wool before it gets to be yarn) combined with macramé cord. Some of the handspun natural wools are very effective, but they're expensive.

Rug yarn. Rug yarn can be either all cotton or cotton mixed with rayon or acrylic. It comes in delightful colors and should be included for wearing apparel (199). It's limp and saggy but generally washable and colorfast. It's difficult to un-knot if you want to correct something, because when you pick out the knot you pick apart the yarn.

The list of knitting and weaving yarns is endless, so be sure to explore all supply sources and experiment with any yarns that appeal to you.

Miscellaneous Cords

In addition to the cords carried in their "Macramé Section" many craft stores also have leather, suede, and plas-

tic lacing. You might want to try very flexible wire, too.

With so many possibilities, the choice of cord for your earlier projects will often hinge on the practical. You should ask yourself three questions: Will it work? Can I get it? What is the cost? Later, when you want a specific effect in a design, familiarity with a variety of cords will be helpful.

Estimating

Sooner or later you're going to have to get involved in arithmetic: it saves you money and time in the end. Like a knitting size gauge, you can develop your own knot gauge. It's easy if you have a variety of graph papers on hand to choose from. A reasonable gauge might consist of eight working cords, their spacing regulated by clove hitching over a horizontal cord (200). Alternating square knots worked tightly would give you both a cords-to-the-inch count and a record of square knot rows to the inch. If you use a measured length to start with, you'll also have a basis for estimating the cutting length required for various other projects in the same cord.

If you make a habit of making knot gauges and labeling the samples as to what they are, where you got the cord, and at what cost, you'll have a good record for planning future projects. Use the cut-off ends when you finish a project to make up a knot gauge (201C). Label these ends and jot down your comments: the material worked well or it didn't handle easily, it made you sneeze, the color came off on your hands, you like the sheen, or you might note that it cuts well with the hot knife. Weeks later, when you want to make a purse, you can go over your notes and select a likely material and you have the knot gauge ready to help you plan everything.

Estimating a Shoulder Bag. Say you want to make a simple shoulder bag, open at the top (201). You decide you want it built to the dimensions shown, worked as indicated (201A). The design is to be mostly alternating square knots, closely spaced with a band of an alternating lark's head pattern. The same motif will be used for the length of the strap. Because a lark's head motif repeated for a strap often includes cords that aren't knotted at all, you decide to work up a sample of that motif with some leftover scraps. Note that the sample shown (201B) includes a full repeat—one right-hand square knot and one left-hand square knot. You find that an 8-strand strap works up to be 3" long. Cords 1 and 8 used 9" for each full repeat. Cords 2 and 7 used 13", 3 and 6 used 6" and 4 and 5 used 3½". These measurements should be quite accurate, because now you want to multiply them by the number of motifs (in this case, twelve) which you'll need to repeat. This gives you the length strap required.

Cut your starting line with 8" to spare for knotting easily (2 x width of bag + 8"). Cut a second cord this length for a clove hitch row if you want it. You need a total of 64 working cords for the front and 64 for the back. Using the

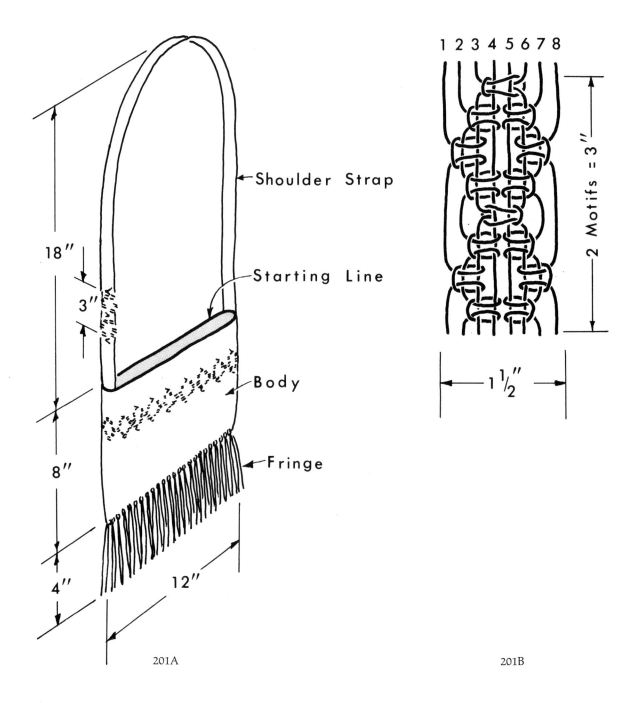

Shoulder Strap

Starting Line

Body

Fringe

18"

3"

8"

4"

12"

201A

1 2 3 4 5 6 7 8

2 Motifs = 3"

1½"

201B

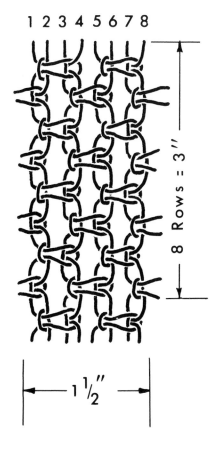

1 2 3 4 5 6 7 8

8 Rows = 3″

1 1/2″

201C

rule of thumb, each cord will be 28″ long. You want a fringe on the bottom so add 4″ for a 3″ fringe, which gives you a working length of 32″. Double that for the cutting length and you get 64″ which is 5′4. Divide the number of working cords in half to get the number of cut lengths required. Take the length of strap cords required and add 64″ to each. You'll need two at 172″, two at 220″, two at 136″, and two at 106″. Total the results and add them to the total footage required for the bag body and you'll have the total footage needed. Divide the number of feet per tube (in this case, 100), and you'll see how many tubes to buy.

There are a number of ways to measure out 64 lengths, each one 5′4″ long. You can buy a fancy warping board or you can set two C-clamps the required distance apart and wind around them. For the odd lengths needed for strap and holding cords, a yardstick and a little care is all that's needed. Make the second cord in each pair the same length as the first.

You'll be starting the strap in the center, so find the center of each cord and pin it to your board. These cords are long enough to tangle a bit and some people will tell you to wind up the excess cord on bobbins or to make a loop held by a rubber band. This does keep the long cords from becoming a mass of entangled ends around your feet, but it means that each bobbin has to be *put* through the knot you're tying, not *pulled* through. If you frustrate easily it's often faster to work standing up, so the cords have a longer way to fall. Then you simply take two or three pulls to get each cord through as you tie.

This process for a simple bag is a good example for any project. Determine the working length of each group of cords as indicated by your knotting plan decision. Always err on the long side: it's easier to cut off extra cord than to splice on when you're short.

9. Embellishments

Embellishments are those things you add to macramé that are made out of materials other than the cord. Some things you add primarily for appearance and others you add for a practical purpose. Useful findings and fittings include handles, fasteners, buckles, and rings manufactured either specifically for use with macramé or adapted by the craftsman to that medium.

You've already seen how small curtain rings can be used to provide a base for a covered ring for hanging or for a drawstring closing. Rings of various sizes and materials also serve as a starting line in many shaped projects. They could, of course, be incorporated for purely esthetic reasons, too, as a sort of bead.

Belt Rings and Buckles

The D-rings sold at needlework and notions counters for fabric belts can be used just as easily for macramé. Start your belt on one D-ring, using the lark's heads to attach the working cords and incorporating the other ring at a reasonable distance from the first one (202). A row of clove hitches to hold the second ring fast is one way to do it.

To use D-rings when you start at the pointed end of the belt, clove hitch around the terminal ring first bringing the cords to the reverse side of the strap. Come back through the strap to the front, then clove hitch on the second ring. Return the cords to the reverse side, tie off, and work the ends in. In wider belts requiring a larger D-ring, you'll need to include some rows of knotting between the two rings to keep them far enough apart to close easily. This D-ring device can also be used if you want a strap on a shoulder bag to be adjustable and aren't satisfied to simply knot the strap for a shorter length. The same principle works with plain rings too if you can't find the D shape in a material you want. You might want plastic instead of the usual brass or steel. Just make sure the ring you select has the strength to stand up under the strain imposed.

Turn-and-Hook Buckle. Macramé can start from both parts of a turn-and-hook-type buckle simply by using lark's heads (203A) to attach your working cords and knotting the cords together at some point in the back of the belt. To start from one end and finish at the other, you have to consider how to duplicate the lark's head look at the finishing end, or you may want to use the clove hitch at both ends which simplifies things. Or, work two or three rows of alternating square knots and fold under the square knotted portion through the buckle, bring the ends through and tie (203B). Finish off the same way at the other buckle part. The double parts will help strengthen

the belt. The objection to this style of buckle is that the macramé is apt to stretch a bit and then the belt no longer fits well unless your design takes this into consideration.

Harness Buckle In selecting a buckle of the harness type, you must first consider its weight in relation to the heft of the cords used. Pick a size that will accommodate a multiple of four working cords. You can again start from the buckle end with lark's heads, but then you have a thickened point or a fringed end to pull through the buckle. You might also start with the pointed end. To attach the buckle, work your belt strap first to the desired length. Turn it face down and lay the buckle in position. Continue the strap through the buckle and fasten off at the backside, having the double thickness under the buckle. To make a built-in belt loop, work the belt from point to buckle as you just did, fold it over the buckle and fasten in the back, finishing off enough strands so that those remaining can be used for the loop (204). If this part is worked in alternating square knots, after you've laid the buckle in place work down to a point, then turn and work at right angles to the belt to make the belt loop right side up. When it's long enough, bring the loop end around, tie off, and work under the remaining ends so the loop aligns with where you started it from.

Leather Buckles. Leather mounted items are another possibility for both belts and bags. Some craftsmen buy or make buckles and punched strap belt fittings, and you may find a similar fitting made for a purse. The macramé parts can be machine sewn to the leather mountings or worked through punched holes.

Block-and-Hook Buckle There are still other types of buckles such as the block-and-hook style. This is a faceplate of one type or another with a hook or pin on the back side for fastening. You can start from the loop and hook into the other end, or start from the pointed end and fasten off at the loop. If you decide to use this type of buckle, be sure you realize how heavy some of them are and select cord that will support them actually as well as visually. Also, the hook can damage some cords if you rely on just hooking into the strap anywhere.

Jewelry Fittings

Necessity, invention, and adaptation are the key words for jewelry fittings. The large-size hooks and eyes sold at notions counters for coats and furpieces make good closures for necklaces and chokers—if you want to start both halves in the back and join them in the front. There are even larger hooks and eyes available from some macramé suppliers. If you work in metal you can make your

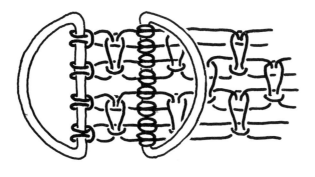

202

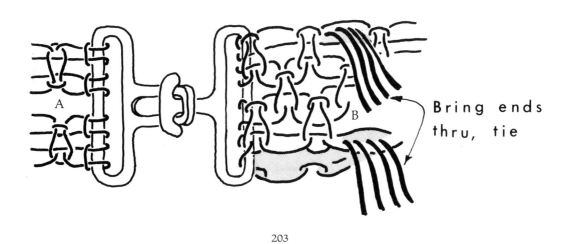

A

B

Bring ends
thru, tie

203

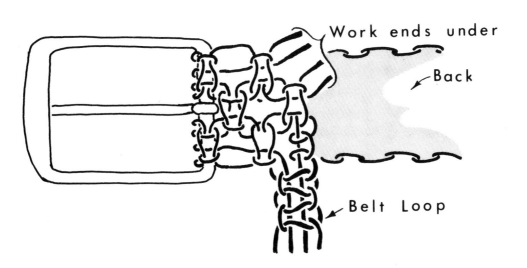

Work ends under

Back

Belt Loop

204

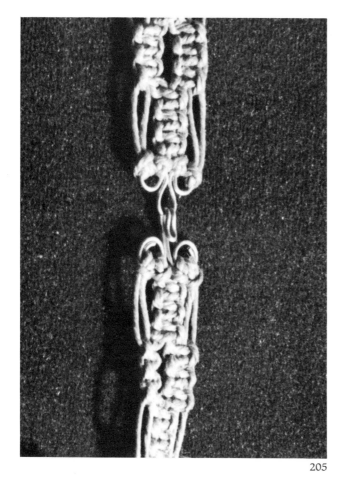

205

206

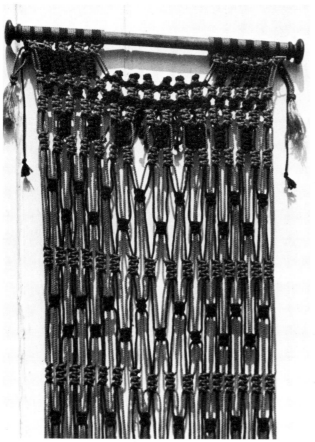

207

208

118 MACRAMÉ

own hooks as shown in this necklace which also uses wire for a design element (205).

Regular jewelry findings are not generally scaled for macramé, though the choker rings that encircle the neck and hook in the back may be used to advantage (206). Some of the larger-sized jumprings might be considered if you are working in very fine cord. Earrings, clips, and pin backs might also be used successfully, depending on the style of the macramé to be mounted.

Handles

Then there are handles: big handles, little handles, ring handles, bar handles, handles meant for tapestry bags, handles meant for fabric bags, or simple handles you can make yourself. When selecting a handle from those offered retail, consider its suitability for the bag design as well as for the cord being used. A dowel, perhaps with a knob on both ends, is the simplest handle you can make if you plan the knotwork so it leaves a space for the fingers to go through (207).

Hoops and Rings. Other items that might be considered functional fittings would include the wooden hoops and metal rings often used to start sculptural hangings or incorporated within hangings. Macramé suppliers offer a larger variety than you'll find rounding up wooden embroidery hoops and Indian dance hoops. You can make your own from reed if you have any handle stock handy. Use a splice joint and wrap it while the glue sets. Or a few loops of soft iron wire covered with drafting tape will suffice if you are going to cover it completely.

Don't neglect your local hardware store. Washers are rings and some hasps can be used for belt and bag closings if filed down first, or some of the brass marine fittings may appeal to you. A lumber or hardware dealer is the place to go for knobs as well as dowels. Some of them also carry the large spindles that are really meant to be furniture parts but make excellent large beads and occasionally may work as a handle.

Beads

Using beads is a whole other bag. You can of course stick a bead on the end of a cord. You can thread on a bead or two anywhere between knots. You can gather two or more strands through a bead. If you add beads in alternating rows you can make a sort of fabric (208). You can use beads for fastenings or you can string beads for a solidly beaded area or strand. A bead can accent the crossed cords of an X or be used as links between sections or between motifs. You can tie an overhand knot below a bead to stop it or you can set it loose on a loop. You can use beads on crossings and string them horizontally into your work. Your imagination and possibly the strength of the bead are the only real limits on how to use beads in a macramé piece.

The problem is finding beads with a large enough hole for the cord to pass through particularly if you want to pass two or more cords through the same bead. Crow beads are about ¼" in diameter and 3/16" long and are made in both ceramics and plastics in a variety of colors and are the most suitable of those beads easily available. The tinier pony beads, meant for bead work, will be usable on very small cord, such as crochet cotton, but the tiniest seed beads are just too small for anything you can see to knot. Going large, you may find barrel beads available, usually in natural, walnut stained, or tinted wood as well as various plastic colors.

The kindergarten wooden beads can be used on some cords. Some of the sources listed offer a variety of barrel and spindle beads in natural or stained wood and some fancy beads of similar shapes and sizes may even be carved. Other importers offer bamboo and tile beads of various sizes. Local potters often make handmade beads with large size holes and some are available by mail order. There is a type of clay that closely resembles the typical red flower pot clay and beads or other ornaments of this material may be just what you're looking for. Or you can make your own beads out of wallpaper rolls, papier-mâché, molded out of wood putty or baker's clay, or you can build them up of wood (209). The Dremel Moto-Tool (an electric carving tool, available at hardware stores) can be used to carve them with, or to shape embellishments from solid wood (210).

Beads that have too small a hole for two cords to pass through may be tied on one cord if you tie an overhand knot with one cord around the beading cord, thread on the bead and tie another overhand knot with the other cord beneath the bead. Threading beads can be done with a needle, or can be done with a looped wire if the doubled cord will go through the bead but the needle won't. Chewing the frayed end of the cord may point it enough to push it through unaided. If you've glued the ends of the cords to keep them from fraying while you work, cut the hardened end on a slant for easier bead stringing. Sometimes the finish inside the bead hole is too rough for easy threading and twisting the bead down on a large blunt needle held securely will often clear the debris.

Other Embellishments

There are many things that can be used as embellishments other than beads. They can be natural things, such as shells or stones, or they can be man-made, such as buttons or bells, or you can make your own.

Shells, Feathers, and Bells. You can buy some shells that already have holes in them or you may want to collect your own shells; however, after cleaning, count on spoiling a few. Some can be drilled with a common bit, but be sure to back up your work so there's no unnecessary strain on the shell. The pressure should go directly through the

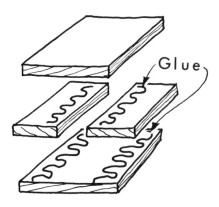

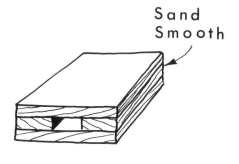

209

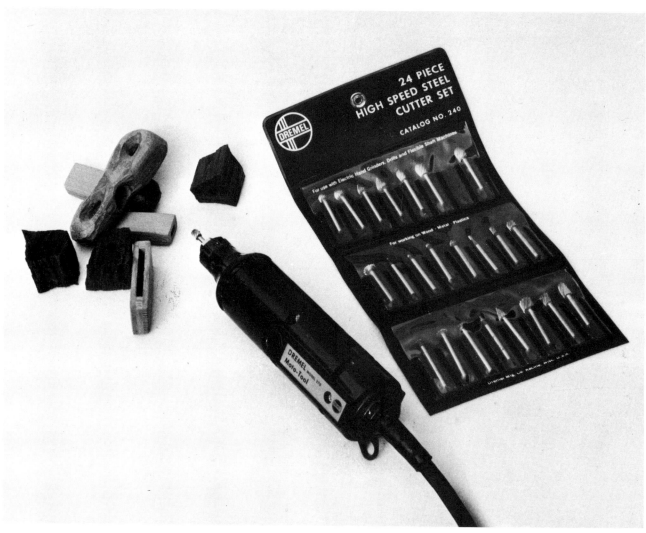

210

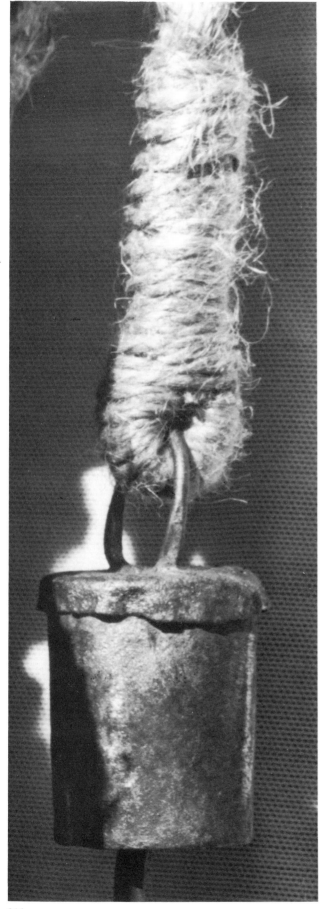

211

212

214. This princess crown was knotted after the cord was stiffened in wallpaper paste (213).

shell into the backup block. Some shells can have a hole ground into them using a high-speed hand power tool with a pointed or shaped grinding point. Others may have to be treated like glass and drilled with kerosene as a lubricant. I've found that a diamond bit (lapidary supply houses have them) in the Moto-Tool does quite well if used with water as a lubricant.

Feathers can be used, too. Sporting goods stores offer some to fishermen, but those packaged for Indian crafts are generally less expensive—or you can go pluck your own. Usually they're attached to macramé by wrapping them onto the ends of the cords.

Bells add a happy note to hangings or decorations. Jingle-bell types can be mounted on a sennit by running the two core cords through the back loop of the bell and back into the continuing sennit. Cowbell styles are better hanging free at the bottom of a sennit and can be attached with a simple knot or you can bend the cord through the bell's loop, back up to form a loop, and then glue and wrap it fast (211). Everything from anodized jingle bells to imported goat bells seems to be available from one source or another if you look around.

Natural Items. While you're looking, don't ignore the beach and nature hikes. Bits of dead wood and driftwood often inspire interesting pieces. Even stones can be incorporated, either by tying them into your macramé or using your ingenuity, as shown in this necklace (212). Epoxy glue was used to hold pairs of smooth stones back to back, providing a groove into which the cords were worked.

Buttons. Don't neglect the button, either, especially the looped-stem types for fastening a belt or purse. One or two of the core cords run through the button loop will hold them and, depending on their size and the knotting pattern, you may or may not need to make a buttonhole. A starting loop can be made to fit a particular button and the button positioned and secured later when you know where to locate it.

Wind Chimes. Wind chimes may be made from any number of pleasant sounding articles—glass, bamboo, shells, or metal pieces. Industrial scrap or other manufactured items are possibilities useful as embellishments—brass curtain rings, for instance, needn't be used as rings but can be included because they look nice.

Making Your Own Embellishments. Making your own embellishments opens up a whole new area. Thin pieces of wood can be strung on cord ends easily enough, or larger solid chunks can be drilled to string like beads. Wooden constructions can be built and the macramé worked in. Wood can certainly be carved and finished nicely for distinctive headings and medallions within a hanging, or can perform more functional chores as bottoms or handles. Some wooden shapes are offered by mail order and may possibly be available from local craftsmen. Pottery medallions as well as beads are available by mail order or you can design a piece to be part of a macramé creation. The same thought holds if you work in glass, wrought iron, plastics, or do copper enameling.

Covering Objects. Another aspect of embellishment is to consider things to cover with macramé such as bottles, pillows, and lampshades. You can glue macramé to a wooden plaque or perhaps a box, gesso the works, and paint or antique it. You can also papier-maché macramé—a point to remember when your costuming duties call for a princess crown overnight. Use soft cotton cable cord and then stiffen the cord with wallpaper paste (213 and 214).

Junk. In antique stores or junk sales you'll often find an interesting bit to start macramé from which is worthless for any other purpose and consequently inexpensive. Sculptural macramé may well be a special branch of junk art: for example, try combining barn siding and rusty parts with jute or cotton cord. The point is to design something that's uniquely yours, freely, easily, and decoratively.

10. Designing

Designing for macramé is very much a matter of personal taste. Some people find long strands and many tassels more attractive than tightly knotted, intricate, repeating patterns. Some people place a higher value on the more traditionally and symmetrically constructed designs (215), while the contemporary artist can find expression in daring selection and deft manipulation of cords (216).

Good macramé has only two basic criteria: the suitability of design and materials, and craftsmanship—keeping an even tension when accuracy is the desired effect; wearing apparel that's comfortable; colors that repeat as intended; ends that don't come untied; headings that carry the weight of the project. In short, an attractive design that reflects the resolution of its construction needs and is worked out with competence.

Macramé as artistic expression is limited only by materials and the imagination of the artist. Macramé as a useful craft is the same, but the project's function must be considered as well. Wall hangings simply hang there and look attractive. The macramé shoulder bag must enclose and protect its contents, hang comfortably from a wide enough strap, open and close securely, and still be attractive.

Your own designs should reflect your originality and creativity. You may delight in the texture of the cords themselves and want only a few knots to give some unity to the piece, or you may prefer to focus on the knotting. You might want little variety in the knotting texture and rely on the color play for interest. Six or eight colors in the leaf pattern may help you keep the knotting straight, but won't bring out the intricacy of the knotted pattern like just one color will. Textural interest can simply be a matter of changing directions in solidly clove-hitched work, but you can accent it with color exchanges, too.

Embellishment is another important element in design, and here compatability is the key. Some cord materials seem to go better with certain embellishments; discriminating selection and practicality are the keys. The large bead with the too-small hole will never look right in a macramé piece. Beads mixed with cords need proportions that are different from beads that are meant to be strung.

The color of both the cord and the embellishment needs to be considered as well as texture. There will be something upsetting about rough, primitive, earth-colored pottery used with colored plastic filament. Scale is also a consideration. A large number of big, wooden beads on slender, delicate cords could be interesting, but the chances are slim.

Suitability must be considered too. Feathers don't wash well and cords that aren't colorfast shouldn't be used for clothing. Cords that fray quickly aren't good choices for belts or other items that need to last.

The weight of embellishments often has a definite effect on your work. One crow bead on the end of a long strand of braided nylon won't do much, but a large iron washer on a strand of jute should hang straight.

Functional fittings must be chosen in the same ways. They must fulfill their duties and still contribute to the overall design of the piece. An extreme example is that a cowboy belt buckle just wouldn't work on a lacy belt.

Planning a Design

In some ways designing can be reduced to the making of a series of decisions. Even a rectangular wall hanging must have its width and length decided eventually. Cords, headings, and embellishments must be selected right along with a decision regarding at least the general style of the knotting to be used. Working freely, each knot becomes another decision.

Some people design down to the last knot on paper first; others make only sweeping general decisions and start knotting, letting the work go its own way. Either approach, or even a path somewhere in the middle, can work.

Sketching on graph paper will allow you to work out your knotting design quite accurately and in considerable detail. It's particularly useful if you want to know how units of one number of cords can be used with units of another, and it's an easy way to keep your arithmetic straight in plotting repeat patterns. If you can buy graph paper in scale with your knotted sample, you can even work quite close to actual size. In general, this approach works best for projects that must meet certain requirements of size and shape. If you try to apply it too faithfully to sculpture, it's apt to be too inhibiting.

With a slightly different technique, graph paper is the easiest way to work out color changes in two-color patterns for solid clove hitching. Here you need only let each square represent one clove hitch. It's not graphic, but you can count.

A freer sketching technique, where only the key elements are indicated may work better for some projects. Take it only as far as necessary to determine a length to cut the cords. This should insure some hope of having enough cord length to complete the intended design. Working this way you're still free to develop your design as you go along. If you make your sketch actual size, you'll be able to use your knotting gauge to estimate very roughly cord length and number of cords to cut, but be generous. It's easier to cut off than to add on.

The absolutely free approach is to simply cut some cords and start knotting, but you must have an idea in

215. (Left) A sampler that combines many types of knots and motifs in a traditional manner.

216. (Above) A hanging combining cloth with stuffed areas and a free protrusion of knotted sennits.

mind to determine which cord to cut and how long to cut it. There is no right way, in fact there is no one way to approach design decisions.

In practical projects it's possible to go a bit further with information and suggest approaches that will work for any number of projects. Five people can take the concept of a slip-over necklace, starting in the center back and finishing at center front. The result should be five completely different pieces, in five different cords, with five different embellishments, in five different color combinations. Each design will be unique and different (217–221).

Wearing Apparel

There's a lot to be said for starting apparel from the shoulders although it's not the only way to do it. Starting with that premise in mind, however, the expandability and cling-fit factors of spaced knotting in a tubular shape make control difficult.

If you have a dressmaker's dummy, that's certainly the easiest way to tackle the project. Indicate on the dummy where you want the piece to start, cover, and finish; then work out a knotting design that will fill it in. Working on a dummy, you would probably start a tubular shape at the bottom of the armholes. You would very likely hang the piece from the shoulders, even if you considered a starting line at the bust and worked up and down from there. You could also start from a line at the waist, work up, and tie at the shoulders too. Don't forget to provide fasteners for a snug waistline or you'll never get the finished project off the dummy.

The next easiest way to work is on a kind of substitute dummy. Buy a dressmaker's pattern for a fabric version of the item you want to make, so shoulder slope, armhole, and neckline can be established. With this information, plus measurements for front and back width at the bustline, you can cut a simple two-faced knotting board on which to knot from the shoulders down and then lace up the side seams when it's finished (222). Or you can build out the front and go tubular at the bottom of the armholes.

For a simple vest or shift that falls straight from the shoulders, you can use a padded coat hanger (223). The shoulder slope is determined by the hanger and the knotting can be done by pinning through to a knotting board or by knotting in-the-air.

A different approach to clothing would be to adapt a printed pattern meant for fabric to macramé. You can knot each piece to the exact shape of the pattern and seam them together as you would a fabric version (224).

This method is best done by taping the pattern parts to large knotting boards and pinning into the pattern to hold your knots in place (225). Running a starting line up one side, across the top, and down the other side gives you a good place to lace your seams to as well as making a smoother outline for each piece. When a dart is indi-

217. This necklace shows an ending of berry knots and wrapping.

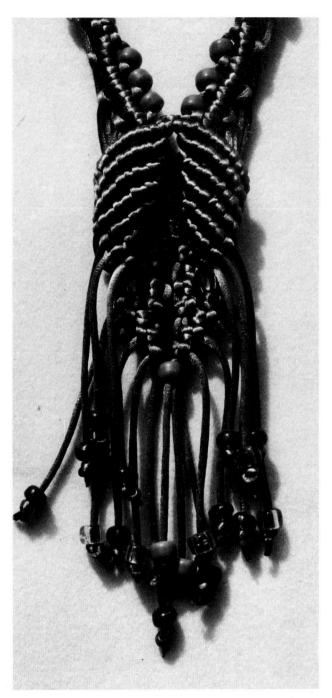

218. A second variation uses hitches and a Josephine knot.

219. Another ending combines a solidly clove-hitched area with square knots and beads.

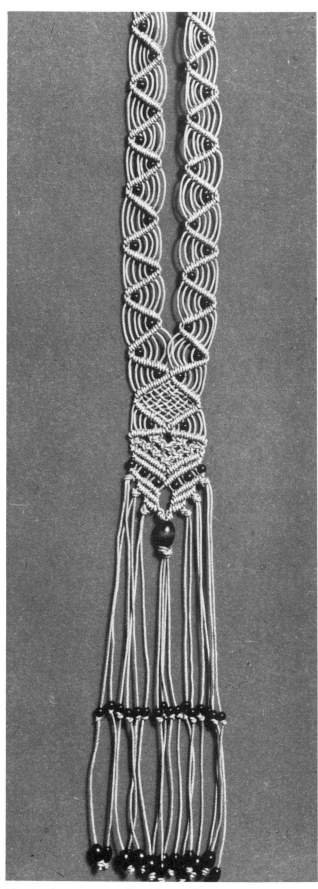

220. This necklace shows stones combined with macramé.

221. Another variation of necklace ending uses hitches, an area of weaving, square knots, and beads.

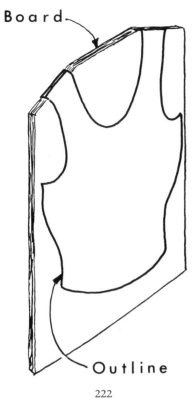

Board

Outline

222

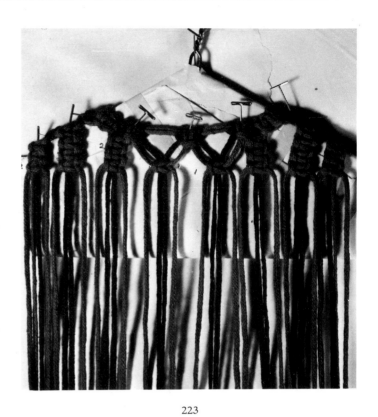

223

224A

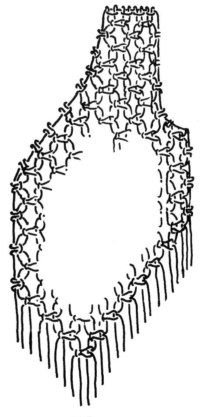

224B

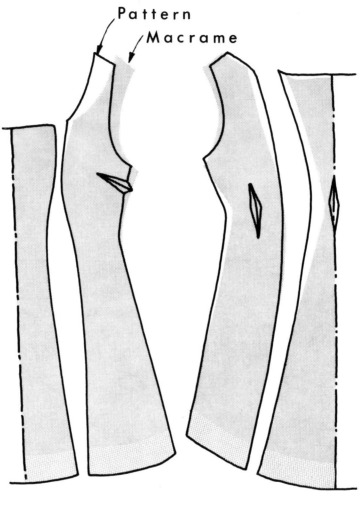

Pattern

Macrame

225

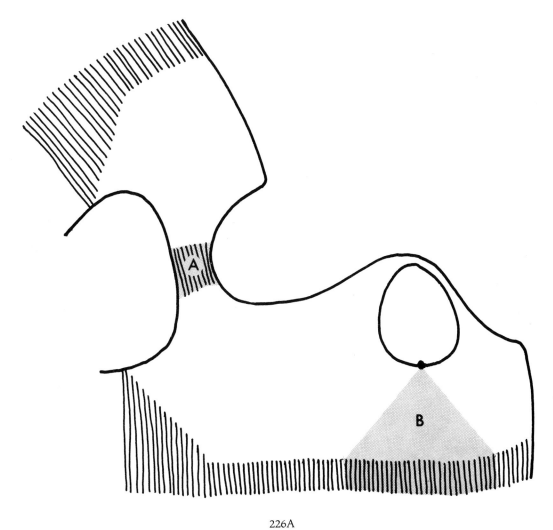

226A

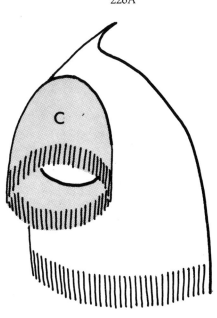

226B

227. Macraméd flowers stand tall in their own pot.

cated, work to the first line of the dart and then move your knotting down to the second line and repin. Then continue knotting. This method works well for fairly compact knotting where the individual pieces will keep their shape when assembled.

The plot-and-assemble method is yet another way (226). Depending on what piece you wish to make, use the strap to cylinder basis of construction to see what combination might make the best sense.

Assemble your printed pattern parts and tape them flat to your knotting board. Pin and knot over them according to the construction plan you have.

For example, for a straight-falling bolero top, assemble the back and front at the shoulders, lay the pattern flat and tape it to your board (226). Starting your straps at the shoulder tops (A), work both ways. Use the outside cord of the straps for the starting line for the armholes and the inside cord of the straps as the starting line for the back neck opening and front edges. Re-pin to work the B areas and add the sleeves at C.

From this illustration you'll see how other construction plans can be used with printed patterns to make a variety of items.

Home Furnishings

The problems of designing macramé are somewhat simpler for home furnishings. You can fill a macramé-covered bottle with sand or plaster for a lamp base. You can also cover a plain lamp shade or work over a wire shade frame and then line it for a decorative shade. You can even make a "flower pot" (227).

Window hangings are simply wall hangings designed with the consideration that the light will be coming through the hanging rather than at it, and this should affect the design you select. Mounting the hanging in the window frame is very easy if you start from a wood strip tacked to the window's head casing. Or you can start from an old window shade roller that no longer rolls, using the brackets already there for a removable window hanging.

The same design considerations go for folding screens, too—light usually comes through them and they must be presentable from either side. One idea worth noting might be to work the panel over dowels set into the screen frame. That way the macramé can be removed for cleaning.

A similar approach can be used for panels set into cabinet doors. Many doors of this style have a lipped opening anyway so you could use the metal frame to work your macramé over and latch it in place as was done originally. If it's an all-wood door, a frame to do the macramé on can easily be attached behind the opening.

Using a wooden or metal frame as a base, it's easy to make a magazine rack, a seat for a camp stool, or a director's chair.

Outdoor uses for macramé of course include planter hangers, but don't rule out making a trellis or stair rail (228) if you have cord treated to take the exposure.

Lining

In soft things like purses and bags, you'll eventually want to consider lining. Select the fabric for the lining so it's compatible with the cord and serviceable for the use it will receive. If the cord is washable, the lining material should be, too. Double-faced rayon taffeta is good for an evening or dress purse where the color of the lining can be seen through the open-knotted design. Seam the lining to fit the style of the bag and the job is just about done.

Felt can be used with jute and other casual string creations. It's easy to use, requiring only a simple seam at the bottom and tacking at the opening edges.

Sail cloth or denim is good strong material and some of the lighter-weight cottons can be used with solidly worked pieces. You'll have to hem the linings around the top edges through, then tack into place.

Sometimes the macramé is actually a panel tacked on top of a completed fabric purse. This is also a good approach when making panels for a dress or vest. Then the macramé is purely decorative and can be tacked to the fabric as often as necessary to hold it in place.

With a drawstring type of bag you have to consider both lining and where you're going to put the drawstring (229). If you put the drawstring in the macramé part then the lining won't gather inside and can be a simple cup shape. Put the drawstring in the lining and tack on the macramé for a different approach. Run the drawstring between the lining and the macramé with two rows of stitching and you can keep them together. The choice depends both on the materials and the design.

Selling Your Work

If you want to sell completed items, you must figure carefully the true cost of the materials first, consider the design in the light of how long it takes you to make 23 more like it, arrive at a unit cost, and then study the market in your area. Can you get twice that for it retail? How much is your time worth?

For example: if it costs you 30¢ for cord, 25¢ for beads, and 5¢ for a hook and eye, but takes you an hour to make one necklace, at $3 an hour, can you get $7.20 retail for that necklace?

After you've decided what items you can make to sell at a reasonable profit, you must find a market for them. Some ladies' shops are anxious to take handmade items on consignment, but naturally won't give you the retail price. You must decide how much you can subtract to get a wholesale price that lets you profit but will still allow enough markup for the store to sell at a competitive retail price.

228. A porch railing loosely filled with square-knotted bailing twine.

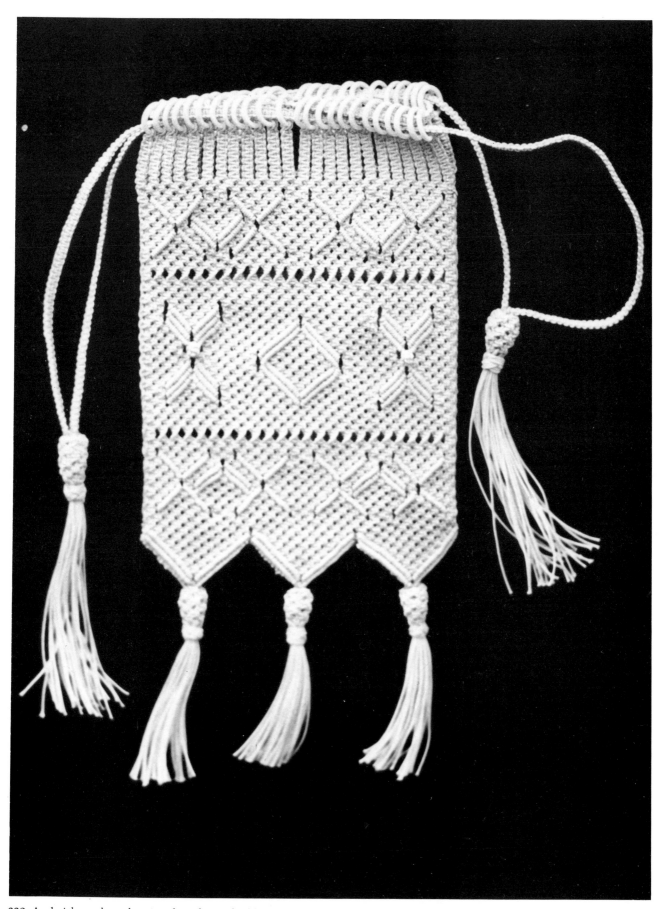

229. An heirloom bag showing densely worked knots and a drawstring top.

Often local craft groups offer selling opportunities at craft fairs and shows. Generally the lower the retail price, the greater the profit; you can sell twelve necklaces at $2.00 each long before you'll sell one hanging at $24.00. Usually the commission you pay the sponsor would be the same—10%, 15% or 25% of the retail price. Don't forget to figure the cost of the time you have to spend sitting and possibly demonstrating with your things at such shows.

Other shows may offer a certain amount of display space for a fee and charge no commission. You have to figure this as cost to determine if it's worthwhile. Can you sell enough at that particular show to make a profit when the additional costs are spread out over the items sold? Some shows charge a space fee plus a commission.

Still other shows are on an invitational basis and may handle the mechanics of selling for you, usually taking a commission for this service. The same arrangement holds for craft groups who have their own store. To sell or not to sell has to be your decision.

You may want to make macramé items as your contribution to charity bazaars. For the sake of good public relations with those who do sell for a living, make sure the prices are reasonably competitive. You are already giving your time and materials to the organization—there's no point in giving them to the customer.

Teaching Macramé

You may find macramé is something you really enjoy doing and want to share that with others, so leading craft groups may be your field. Do teach approach rather than copy. It's all the better if each project is completely unlike anything else and this feature of macramé works to advantage in dealing with group crafts.

There's no reason macramé cannot be used in summer camps or in recreation rooms for the elderly and it has become a part of textile and art classes at every level. There is no premium on getting done first nor on imitating the sample perfectly.

In camps, the leader can convince the slow ones to work simply, while the speedy kids tie more knots. With the elderly, those that see well can do fine work while those with visual and coordination problems can find enjoyment in large loosely tied hangings of multiple colors or variegated textures. The possibility of group projects (one project, a number of knotters) is also worth investigating in some situations.

Calling macramé "square knotting" and stressing fancy knot work as a sailor's pastime removes the "girl's work" enough to interest boys and men in the craft.

Painting by numbers does not result in great works of art. Knotting to the pattern does not create original macramé pieces. *Do your own thing!*

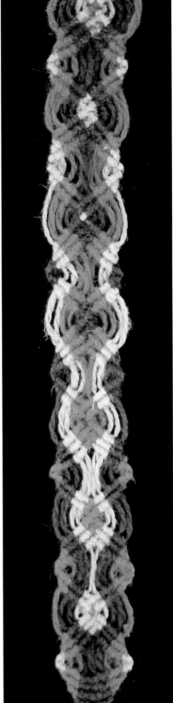

Belt (above), by the author. The simple device of using clove-hitched crosses with two bars on top, three on the bottom, automatically shifts the colors and provides the pattern in this jute belt. Photo, Lawrence L. Schroth, Jr.

Purse (left), by Anthony E. Kropilak. Leather provides a base for the macraméd and crocheted purse of braided cotton cord accented with wooden beads.

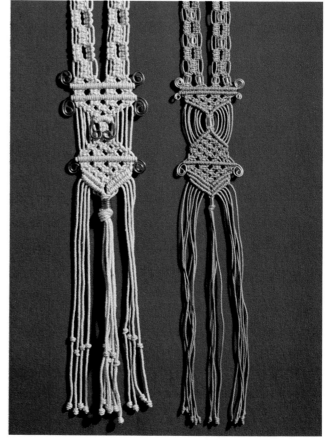

Round Shield *(above), by the author. Red rayon twine and white nylon braid were square knotted from the outside of the circle to the center, then turned loose to fall singly and in sennits decorated with knots, beads, and feathers.*

Etter Green Purse *(above right), designed by the author for* **Lady's Circle Magazine***. Horizontal rows of clove hitching set off diagonally hitched repeats in this simple purse made with jute cord and lined with felt. Courtesy* **Lady's Circle Magazine***. Photo, Geoffrey Clements.*

Copper and Silver Necklaces *(right), by Anthony E. Kropilak. Both necklaces incorporate fittings and features made of wire and metal tubing. Photo, Geoffrey Clements.*

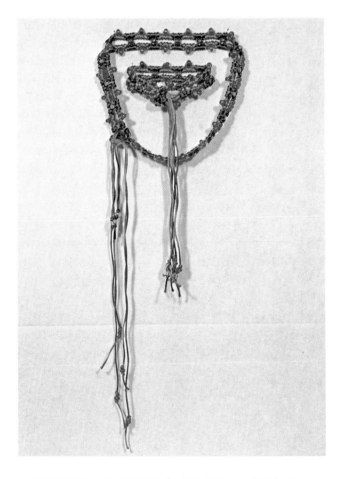

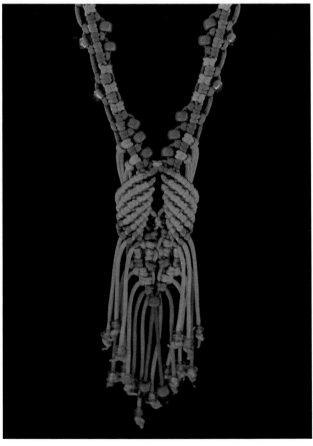

Jute Hanging *(above), by the author. This multi-layered, circular hanging of 5-ply and 2-ply jute starts from rings and ends in tassels and Pakistani bells hung on wrapped loops. The bottom bell drops from an 8-strand braid decorated with Turk's heads.*

Etter Choker and Sash *(above left), designed by the author for* **Lady's Circle Magazine**. *Rayon rattail and beads knotted in a simple lark's head repeat design make an attractive accessory set. Courtesy* **Lady's Circle Magazine**. *Photo, Geoffrey Clements.*

Purple Necklace *(left), by the author. This slip-over necklace takes on a three dimensional look because of the simple twist in the otherwise solidly clove-hitched area. It was worked in rayon rattail and jewel-like beads. Photo, Lawrence L. Schroth, Jr.*

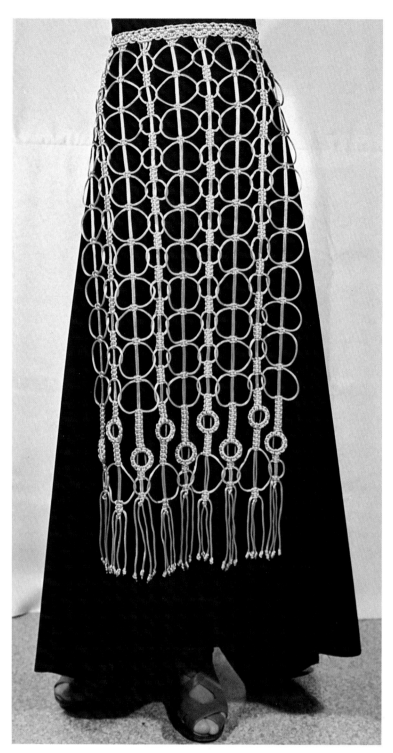

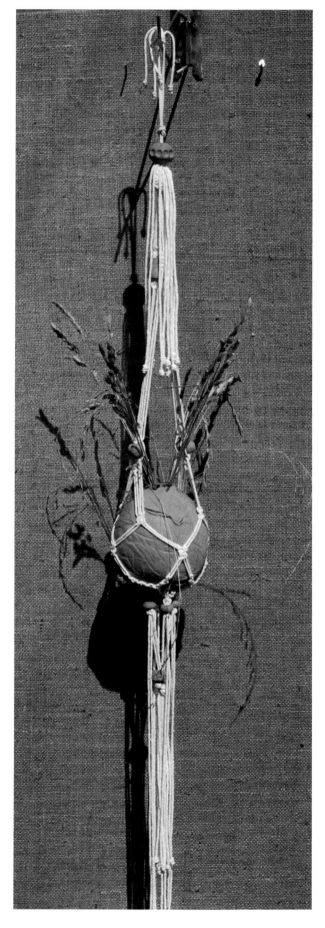

Apron *(above), by the author. Butterfly knots in one sennit link loosely with those in the adjoining sennits. Photo, Geoffrey Clements.*

Weed Pot *(right), by Anthony E. Kropilak. Restraint with macramé allows the weeds and pot to become the focus of this hanging.*

Log Tote *(opposite page, left), by the author. Brown and orange nylon braid was used to make this expandable tote. The color exchange provides the striped effect. Photo, Geoffrey Clements.*

Hanging with Pottery Pieces *(opposite page, right), by Anthony E. Kropilak. Pottery is combined with macramé worked in jute cord in this imaginative hanging. Photo, Lawrence L. Schroth, Jr.*

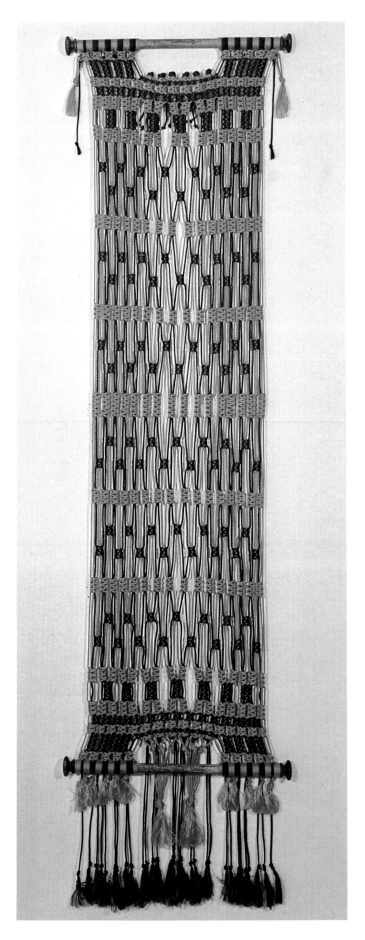

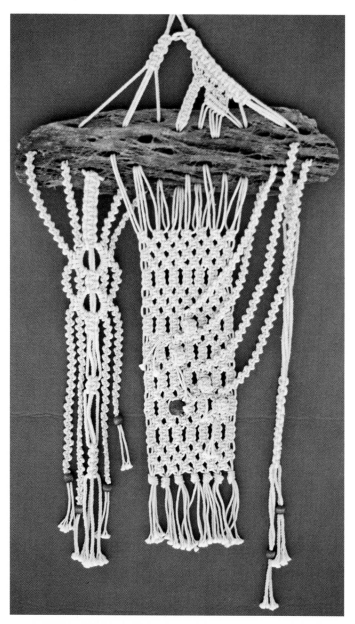

Hanging with Cactus *(above), by the author. The location of the openings in the piece of dried cactus suggested the multi-layered form of this wall hanging. The cactus also contrasts nicely with the cotton seine cord.*

Bowl Hanger *(right), by the author. Square-knotted sennits of jute mailing twine were started on a ring and finished with a wrapped tassel incorporating orange wooden beads.*

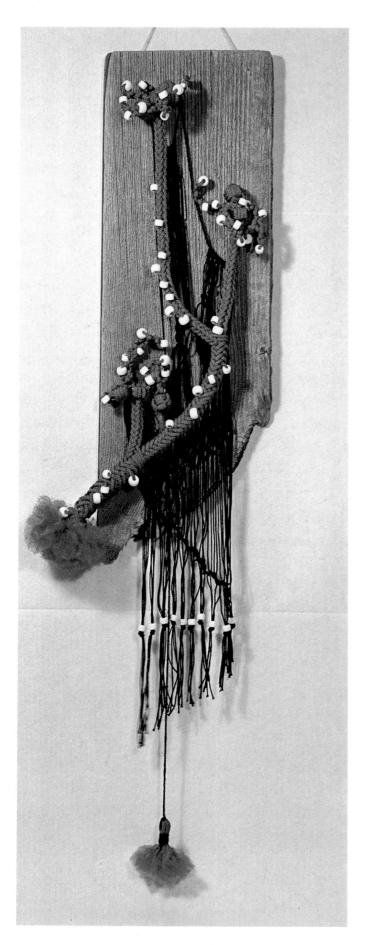

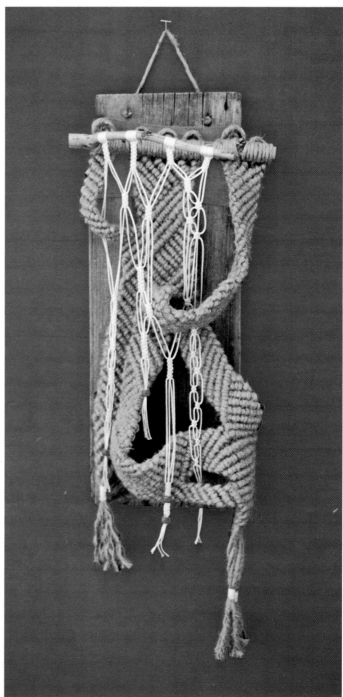

Wall Hanging *(above), by the author. A branch attached to a piece of barn siding provides textural interest in this three-dimensional hanging. It was worked in clove-hitched, 5-ply jute and square-knotted nylon braid.*

Hanging with Wood *(left), by the author. Found objects and weathered barn siding are enhanced by several areas and colors of macramé and by two sizes of white plastic beads. Steam was used to puff out the tassels. Photo, Geoffrey Clements.*

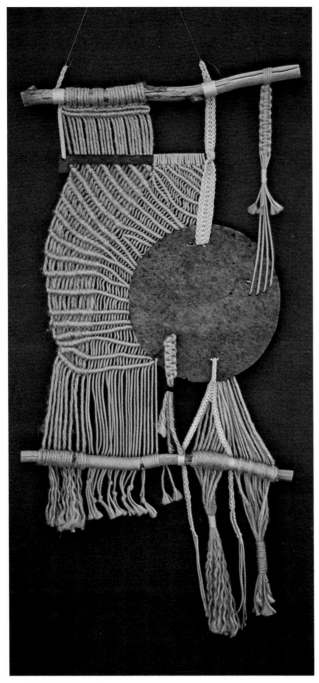

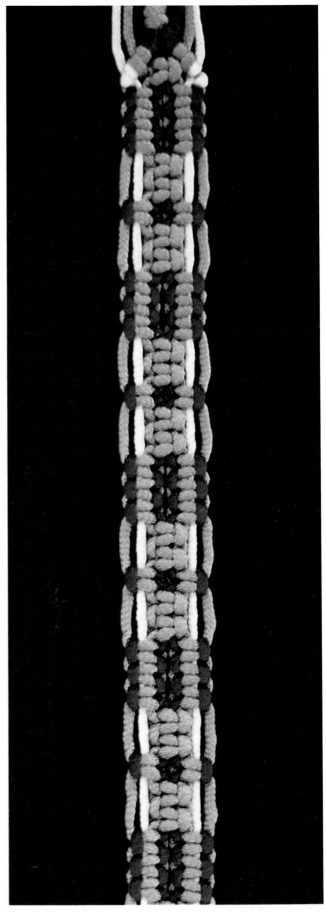

Yellow Wall Hanging *(above), by the author. Holes were drilled into the piece of rusty tin to support the wavy clove-hitched lines of jute and nylon and the strap of lark's heads worked in cotton. Photo, Laurence L. Schroth, Jr.*

Belt *(right), by Anthony E. Kropilak. Alternating square knots and controlled color exchanges provide the interesting pattern in this belt worked in two shades of braided cotton cord. Photo, Lawrence L. Schroth, Jr.*

Credits

Black and White Photos

9. Designed and worked by Anthony E. Kropilak.
26. Designed and worked by Augusta Baum.
30. Designed and worked by Anthony E. Kropilak.
69. Collection of Doris Hupp, Stillwater, New Jersey.
76. Collection of the P. C. Herwig Co., New York.
118. Designed and worked by Anthony E. Kropilak.
131. Worked by Christian Svensen of the Seaman's Church Institute.
178. Worked by Trudy Duff.
205, 206, 208. Designed and worked by Anthony E. Kropilak.
212, 219. Designed and worked by Jennifer Place.
215. Designed and worked by Gretchen Brierley.
216. Designed and worked by Anthony E. Kropilak.
217. Designed and worked by Gretchen Brierley.
221. Designed and worked by Anthony E. Kropilak.
227. Designed and worked by George Pfiffner.
228. Designed and worked by Sharon Morgenweck.
229. Collection of the P. C. Herwig Co., New York.

All other pieces photographed were designed and worked by the author.
Credits for works shown in color are included in the captions.

Suppliers List

Columbia-Minerva Corp.
295 Fifth Avenue
New York, New York 10016
Mail order address:
Columbia-Minerva Corp.
Box 500
Robesonia, Pennsylvania 19551
Limited macramé cords, beads, and fittings available through specialty shops and art needlework departments.

Frederick J. Fawcett, Inc.
129 South Street
Boston, Massachusetts 02111
Wide range of fine, linen weaving threads in great colors available by direct mail order.

Gloria's Glass Garden
Box 1990
Beverly Hills, California 90213
Retail or mail order, free catalog
Offers a special line of handmade ceramic beads, porcelain and stoneware for macramé, and all types of fancy glass beads.

Gray Owl Indian Craft Co., Inc.
150-02 Beaver Road
Jamaica, New York 11433
Mail order catalog is 25c.
Beads, feathers, and shells primarily for Indian crafts.

Hartford Cordage & Twine Co., Inc.
175 Park Ave.
East Hartford, Connecticut 06108
Manufacturer of cotton, jute, sisal, nylon cords, boards, and T pins for retail sales. Their cotton cable cord is dyed all the way through.

P. C. Herwig Co., Inc.
264 Clinton Street
Brooklyn, New York 11201
Catalog is 50c.
The square knot headquarters, formerly located in the Brooklyn Navy Yard. They have a balanced selection of cords and fittings and a variety of glass, wooden, stoneware, and bamboo beads.

Knit & Knot Shop
2701 North 21st.
Tacoma, Washington 98406
Color cards are $1.00.
A variety of cords, beads, fittings, and bells.

Knit Services, Inc. (The Macramé Studio)
281 East Kelso Road
Columbus, Ohio 43202
Catalog is 25c, color cards are $2.00.
An excellent variety of cords and fittings, as well as beads and cold water dyes.

Lily Mills Company
Shelby
North Carolina 28150

Color samples are 25c.

Colorfast cords in nylon, cotton, and polypropylene made especially for macramé, available through art needlework departments, specialty shops, and by direct mail order.

Macramé & Weaving Supply Co.
63 East Adams Street
Chicago, Illinois 60603

Free catalog, $1 for color samples (50c refundable).

Full range of cords, beads, and fittings, including natural seeds and shells drilled for beading, bells, and rings.

Mike Consumer Products
(an Indian Head company)
P.O. Box 398
Anniston, Alabama 36201

A line of cords, including a nylon-cotton mix, made just for macramé and available through hardware and housewear sections and some specialty shops.

Warp-Woof Potpourri
514 N. Lake
Pasadena, California 91101

Catalog with some samples is 50c. Mail order only.

A large variety of cords, beads, fittings, natural feathers, dyes, and shells. Handfinished walnut pieces to start hangings from.

Weavers Loft
320 Blue Bell Road
Williamstown, New Jersey 09094

Free catalog, 50c for sample card.

A variety of cords, including a number of jutes, and a limited number of beads and fittings.

Wellington Puritan Mills, Inc.
(Arlington Products)
Madison, Georgia 30650

Braided nylon and cotton cords in a range of colors and sizes, available through retail outlets, hardware, houseware, and marine stores.

Knotting board material, Homasote, is available from most local building materials dealers in 4′ x 8′ sheets, easily cut to size.

The *Dremel Moto-Tool* and the *Weller Hot Knife* are available in some hardware or tool supply stores, or can be ordered directly from the manufacturers:

Dremel Mfg. Co.
4915 21st. Street
Racine, Wisconsin 53403

Weller Company
The Cooper Group
Box 728
Apex, North Carolina 27502

T Pins (also called bankpins) are available through stationery and notions stores.

British Suppliers

Most hardware stores, farm suppliers, stationers, shop-blind makers, sail makers, and chandlers stock a very wide range of threads, strings, etc. You can find these places in directories or while wandering around different small towns. Yachting shops and sports shops have a lot of nylon and other ropes and cords, and in small fishing villages you can usually find a store with all sorts of string. For the more delicate threads, the haberdashery departments in all large stores have various things which can be used.

Fred Aldous Limited
The Handicraft Centre
37 Lever Street
Manchester 1

The Bead Shop
53 South Molton Street
London W1

Arthur Beale
194 Shaftsbury Avenue
London WC2
All kinds of ropes, nylon cords, twines, and strings.

Bourne & Hollingsworth Limited
Oxford Street
London W1

Dryad (Handicrafts) Ltd.
Northgates
Leicester LEi 40P
A fine natural Macramé twine in ½ lb. balls. They only accept postal orders at a minimum value of £2.

D.H. Evans & Co., Ltd.
318 Oxford Street
London, W1

Ells & Farrier Limited
5 Princes Street
London W1
Will send by post if you know what you want.

Hugh Griffiths
"Brookdale"
Beckington
Bath
Somerset
Vast selection of weaving yarns and threads.

MacCullock & Wallis Limited
25-26 Dering Street
London W1
Sells boxes of piping cord which is more economical than buying it in stores by the yard. They have various thicknesses.

Mace & Nairn Limited
89 Crane Street
Salisbury
Wiltshire
Offers an excellent postal service for various threads, cords, gold threads, etc.

M. Mallock & Sons
44 Vauxhall Bridge Road
London SW1

Mersey Yarns
(Margaret Stagroat)
2 Straplands Road
Liverpool L14 3LD
Loom cord, heddle twine, macramé twine in colours.

The Needlewoman Shop
146-148 Regent Street
London
They have various threads, yarns, and rug wools, and also a fine macramé twine in colours.

Nottingham Handicraft Co.
Melton Road
West Bridgford
Nottingham NG2 6HD
For schools, colleges, etc., but will send packages for the public also. They have various cottons, cords, etc.

Sesame Ventures
(A L M Kemp)
New Invention
Dulverton
Somerset, Dulverton 216
They have a good selection of wooden beads.

Annotated Bibliography

Andes, Eugene *Practical Macramé*. London, Studio Vista Ltd.; New York, Van Nostrand Reinhold Co., 1971. A pattern book with some very imaginative ideas.

Ashley, Clifford, W. *The Ashley Book of Knots*. London, Faber & Faber, Ltd., 1967.

Boy Scouts of America *Knots and How To Tie Them*. New Brunswick, New Jersey, Boy Scouts of America, 1965. Practical knots you'll want to know sooner than you think.

Coats, J. and J.P. *Anchor Manual of Needlework*. London, B.T. Batsford, Limited, 1968.

Fisher, Joan. *The Art of Macramé*. London, Hamlyn Group, 1972.

Harvey, Virginia I. *Macramé: The Art of Creative Knotting*. New York, Van Nostrand Reinhold Co., 1967. Materials, tools, and techniques; a full treatment and a good basic book.

Harvey, Virginia I. *Color and Design in Macramé*. New York, Van Nostrand Reinhold Co., 1971. An expanded treatment of color and design aspects accompanied by good technical information and inspiring illustrations.

Herwig, Philip C. (editor) *Square-Knot Book No. 1, No. 2, and No. 3*. Brooklyn, New York, P. C. Herwig Co., 1926. Square knot headquarters formerly in the Brooklyn Navy Yard, this company shows the belt and bag designs typical of Navy projects done for diversion, not necessity.

Kroncke, Grete *Mounting Handicraft*. New York, Van Nostrand Reinhold Co., 1967. This handbook on what to do with completed art needlework is very helpful in showing how to utilize macramé to greater advantage.

Meilach, Dona Z. *Macramé: Creative Design in Knotting*. New York, Crown Publishers, 1971. A most inspiring book on sources and ideas for designs and forms—includes sculptural macramé and mixing materials.

Meilach, Dona Z. *Macramé Accessories*. New York, Crown Publishers, 1972. A paperback pattern book that includes additional project suggestions.

Puritan Mills *Rope, Knots, Hitches, and Splices*. Louisville, Kentucky, Puritan Mills, Inc., 1968. A clearly illustrated reference book for knots and techniques related to any practical use of rope, including macramé.

Phillips, Mary Walker *Step-by-Step Macramé*. New York, Golden Press, 1970. Complete beginners guide to the craft.

Shaw, George R. *Knots: Useful and Ornamental. New York, Collier Books*, The Macmillian Co., 1972. A step-by-step instruction book for decorative and useful knotwork.

Short, Eirian. *Introducing Macramé*. New York, Watson-Guptill Publications; London, B.T. Batsford, 1972.

Torbet, Laura *Macramé You Can Wear*. New York, Ballantine Books, Watson-Guptill Publications, 1972. A pattern book of clothing or accessory projects.

Walker, Louisa *Graded Lessons in Macramé Knotting and Netting*. New York, Dover Books, 1971. Originally published in 1896, this book is interesting from a historical point of view, but the authoritarian directions given reflect the attitude.

Index

Edited by Jennifer Place
Designed by James Craig and Robert Fillie
Set in 10 point Elegante by Publishers Graphics, Inc.
Printed and bound in Japan by Dai Nippon Printing Company